THOSE MOMENTS
THAT MATTER

as angels dance among the demons

on the broad ways of our lives

MARY JANE HOLT

Copyright © 2020 Mary Jane Holt

All rights reserved.

ISBN: 9798568989509

With gratitude for many
who have been there more than most
to help celebrate or just survive those moments
that seem to have mattered more than most,
I now share parts of my grace laced story.

INTRODUCTION

On these pages I will share truth – measured truth to some degree, but still as unadulterated as I am able to tell it while referencing angels in the midst of demons dancing on the many broad ways of our lives as our most extraordinary moments that matter tick away. I hope to raise awareness about the activity of the spirit realm.

At this writing, I am 72 years old and I find that the questions still rule. For instance, I am puzzled about the difference between being thankful to or towards God, and simply worshipping God. I am indeed thankful for where God has brought me from, and where I could have been on countless occasions, were it not for His grace and mercy. He has walked and talked with me and loved me so well on my earth journey. But have I and do I praise God well? I do not know. I think I do not know how to do that - to properly praise God.

What I do know is that I must tell my stories and help you tell yours as well, because He is in them. God is there on every page of our lives, in every sentence, begging us to use commas where needed, put periods into sentences that run on too long, move on to the next paragraph, and jump to the next chapter when it is time. He is actively loving, caring, and ever longing for us to acknowledge His Presence, talk with Him more often, and appreciate His insight and guidance more appropriately, as we make our way back to Him. ~mjh

THOSE MOMENTS THAT MATTER

CHAPTER ONE

It is May 29, 2020 as I start to piece together a few highlights of my personal story. I was quite distraught early today, so very sad, as I listened to the memorial service for Ravi Zacharias and was forced to imagine a world without him and his many answers.

I only met Ravi one time, but it was enough for me to know that this man, with whom God clearly walked, had been born to make a difference in many lives. In life and in death he sure made a difference in mine. When I met him, I had heard him speak briefly at a press conference that I was covering and after he had finished talking, the floor was opened for questions. My question to Ravi probably was not a fit for that setting; nevertheless, I longed to ask it, so I did.

I do not remember my exact wordage, but for many long years I have fretted over people praying for others and telling them that they are going to be healed - that they just know they will be. Sometimes they even say, "If your faith is great enough you will be healed." Then the suffering soul walks away with more guilt piled on top of his or her pain, anguish, or weakness. They walk away believing their lack of faith is so great that they do not deserve healing. So I asked Ravi, "What happens …

what do we do to people when we tell them that we've prayed for them, and we know they're going to be healed, and it does not happen?"

Interestingly, Ravi's entire demeanor changed. I watched a man, instantly and literally, look into my heart and speak from his heart. He told me of his own chronic back pain and how excruciating it had been and how he had prayed for relief for many years, and that others had prayed as well. To some extent he had experienced what had always bothered me. Then one day - I do not recall the name of the man he mentioned - but one day, he said a man came to see him, and that man told him that he wanted to pray for him, specifically for his back pain. He prayed and the pain went away that day. After many long years of unanswered prayers, there finally was an answer. A reprieve from the pain was granted for a time.

I was in awe of the man, Ravi Zacharias, when we parted. I later thought of hundreds of questions that I would have so very much enjoyed asking him, but that was my only interaction. A few months back when I read that he would not be at an event, which I once more would be covering and where he was to be a keynote speaker, I discovered that he would not be there because of back pain. During the treatment of that back pain it was learned that he had cancer, and in a very few short nights he died on May 19th.

Today, on May 29th, there was a celebration of his life, a memorial that was aired on YouTube. I muted my phones then sat quietly and listened to speaker after speaker, and finally, when you would think there could be no more surprises left, they closed the service by asking Lecrae, perhaps the most famous rapper in the world at this time, to come to the stage. He spoke of how he and Ravi had been working on a rap song, and then he closed the service by rapping, after which I was even more acutely stricken with grief because as Lecrae started to leave the stage he said, "Now the man with all the answers gets to ask his questions."

I am not a woman who has a lot of answers. I never have been. I have always had more questions, but my questions have been honest, and they have led me well. I'm okay with the path I've had, with the journey, with my experiences. I remember hearing my older son say something one day that cut to the core at the time. Later I owned it though because it was truth. He was talking, remembering, hurting, discussing past deeds, experiences, relationships and, at that time in life, he and his dad were struggling. Their relationship was strained. He was describing his dad and trying to focus on his father's positive attributes, and then he spoke of me, and said, "You mom, you're just all over the place." I did not expect to hear that.

I am, however, a searcher, a seeker and I change a lot. I try to embrace who I am on any given day. As much as my son's words hurt me that particular day, it was not too long afterwards when I heard his father, my husband of more than 40 years, said something about me to somebody that I took it to be the greatest compliment I'd ever heard. He said, "The only consistent thing about my wife is her inconsistencies." Immediately, I suspected my son and my husband probably were saying the same thing. Yet one had made me want to cry and one had made me smile with joy.

When my son said what he did, I knew I did not have all the answers. I felt impotent, like I had failed him by not being consistent in my words and beliefs. When my husband said it, I felt acceptance, joy in being recognized for the reality of who and what I am. First and foremost, on any given day, I think of myself as a woman with far more questions than answers, and I am okay with that. I am drawn to life's contrasts, to the unexplainable, and to a measure of as much truth (whatever is true in any given moment on any given day) as my earth mind and frame can process.

As I type these words, in an attempt to share some of my life experiences along with a few personal truths in this memoir, I must confess that I am "jealous of the angels" around the throne today with

Ravi and Jesus and God ... and my husband. For at this point, in this realm, I suspect I shall always have more questions than answers. There is no rhyme or reason, no preconceived notions, no outline regarding what I shall share with you in this "memoir of sorts"; I will simply let the words fall where that may.

(Jealous of the Angels was written by Canadian singer/songwriter Jenn Bostic. Buy it. Listen!)

CHAPTER TWO

In 2003, I reached out to every reachable friend of my high school graduating class as I started planning a class reunion. It was not a significant anniversary year. I had been subconsciously aware of an almost spiritual need to do it the previous year when I had been gravely ill. In February, I let the desire become a conscious one, and with my friend Andrea's support, put wings to it.

Among those I called early on was a woman I considered my best friend from age 14 thru 17. We had reconnected several times over the years. On the day I made the call to talk about the planned reunion my friend, Cindy, informed me that it had been a decade since we had spoken. "I bet you don't remember what you said to me during our last conversation, do you?"

I confessed that I did not and was pretty sure from the sound of her voice that she was about to tell me, so I went ahead and asked.

She said, "You told me that I needed to get a life, then you hung up on me."

Oops.

The memory of that conversation came rolling in. She was correct. Oh, yeah, I remembered. Indeed, I suddenly and quite clearly remembered.

Then she said, "Well, I did."

'You did what?"

"I got a life."

"Tell me about it."

"Do you really want to know?" she asked.

Yes, I really wanted to know!

She continued, "I divorced my last husband (her fourth), bought my own home, and I planted my own garden."

She was alluding to something I had shared with her years before, a poem written by **Veronica Shoffstall**. This is it:

After a While
by Veronica Shoffstall

After a while you learn
the subtle difference between
holding a hand and chaining a soul,
and you learn that love doesn't mean leaning
and company doesn't mean security,
and you begin to learn that kisses aren't contracts
and presents aren't promises,
and you begin to accept your defeats
with your head up and your eyes ahead,
with the grace of a woman,
not the grief of a child,
and you learn to build all of your roads on today

because tomorrow's ground is too uncertain for plans,
and futures have a way of falling down in mid-flight.
After a while you learn that even sunshine burns
if you get too much.
So you plant your own garden
and decorate your own soul,
instead of waiting for someone to bring you flowers.
And you learn that you really can endure...
That you really do have worth.
And you learn and you learn...
With every goodbye you learn.

The author once told me that the guy about whom she wrote that poem really was not worth the paper and ink it took to pen the words which have now been shared all over the world.

So, Cindy had gotten a life! All her own! And she clearly was proud of herself and happy to be telling me about it. Then ... as I found myself rejoicing with her ... as I eagerly drank in every word, she suddenly said, "Now I'm dying."

I thought, "Seriously, you tell me you have a beautiful life you have made for yourself, that you love it, and now you are losing it," but I stayed silent and let her talk.

She was indeed preparing to lose it. Her breast cancer was back again and with a vengeance. This time it had metastasized, and her bones were brittle and breaking. She was entertaining her hospice options. As she talked, I suspected that a most extraordinary year was about to unfold. The famed words of the Welsh poet, Dylan Thomas, assured me during that initial conversation about the reunion, that Cindy "would not go gentle into that good night." She did not disappoint! She could not.

Cindy and I would never have been friends had we not lived in rural Georgia and been required to ride a school bus for an hour one way to school. I am the oldest of seven kids. I was, even at 14, the forever responsible one with a deep desire to be in control of myself and as much of my environment as possible. The now thriving free spirit in me today that often wrestles with the more dominant side of my personality is probably a direct result of my knowing and loving Cindy. She was spontaneous and carefree. Impossible to contain. Beyond control. If she wanted to do it, she did it.

We often imagined other worlds and other realities as we played together in the woods and back roads and clear rippling streams of South Georgia. Many nights, we would cook over an open wood fire in her backyard. We doubled dated. We shared secrets. Many. I drove her to some of her romantic excursions with one of her high school teachers. To this day, I have no idea who seduced whom. I know she never hated any of her lovers. Kinda like that Lacy J Dalton song about "Me and These Arms" loving every man that they held. Cindy freely lived and loved well in all of the moments that mattered in her life. I will be eternally grateful for the ways she tried to teach me to do the same. I am still learning, but I suspect that I will never have a better teacher than Cindy this side of eternity.

I like to think I rubbed off on her a little bit as well. Throughout the years I knew her, she nurtured several personalities definitely more than two. We talked about them during her last year of life. I even gave her a paperweight with three cobalt blue dolphins that looked like they were gleefully jumping in crystal clear water. "Representative of your three more dominant personalities," I told her. She laughed gleefully and hugged me hard!

One of my first steps in planning for the class reunion in October of 2003 was to compile a list of questions for all class members. I planned to custom publish a book containing the answers I received. Randall was the first classmate to respond. He also came to the reunion. It was the first one he had ever attended. After high school he had gone out into the new world of computer technology and made a name and fortune for himself in the software industry. He always was quiet, kinda shy. None of us knew that the reason he spent a lot of time in his hotel room was because he was sick. Dying. A few months later, the little book, with the published answers he gave to questions I had asked, was used to write his eulogy.

My life was quite poignantly impacted that year by many former schoolmates, but there was no greater influence than what Cindy had over me. She eagerly answered her questions, and her responses sparked many late night conversations which caused me to remember well why I had hung up on her a decade earlier, the night I told her to "get a life."

Cindy was addicted to romance, alcohol, and church during most of her life. She was always quite open with me about all three in that order, although I think church came first and was replaced by God being first in the end. The alcohol consumption did not make her sleepy. Not ever. It turned her on and she wanted late night conversations. Not starting at 10 or 11 pm, but usually at midnight and running until 3 and 4 a.m. A decade earlier, I was publishing a health magazine and needed my sleep so I could be alert and work well during the day, so I could not handle all-nighters. We had enjoyed several trips into the North Georgia and North Carolina mountains. She visited me a few times and I visited her in her South Georgia home a couple of times. That was a bit uncomfortable because she was bound and determined to get me to watch her porn flicks. She had quite a collection. I always wondered what happened to them after her death, but never asked. During her last year, I did once ask what she was going to do with them before her death. She did not show any interest in destroying them. Oh, well, while porn was never my cup of tea, it clearly was hers, and I feel honored to have been let in on all sides of Cindy. She never bored me. I loved her dearly. Still do.

That said, as 2003 unfolded and Cindy and I began reminiscing in preparation for both the class reunion and her impending death, well... she was still a night owl! She *still* wanted to talk from midnight until 3 a.m. This time I felt guilty about saying no because, after all, she was dying, and she wanted me to help her figure out how to do it. Yep, *how to die,* specifically, how to face God, in light of her extraordinarily colorful personal history. One night she called at her usual time and we talked long. Too long. At 8 a.m. I had to be in Newnan, GA to interview a cardiologist from Duke who was in town talking about alternative medicine. I was no longer publishing the health magazine, but I was still writing my column and I wanted an in-depth conversation with this physician. However, even though I made the 8 a.m. appointment, I was not to have a real conversation with the guy.

Some folks are not good at that - even the highly educated and brilliant type which he clearly was. He had a well-practiced speech, more or less, that he liked to deliver in a well-practiced sequence. If I interrupted him with a question he just started over and limited himself to what he came to say, and real conversation never happened.

That does not happen to me often. I don't make small talk. Nor do I listen well to lectures. I like open honest discussion and I love questions, even the unanswered ones, maybe even especially the unanswered ones. I have always believed some questions to be more honest than answers.

As I drove home from that frustrating interview, I recalled how Cindy once more had kept me awake into the wee hours of that morning and I knew that I must put a stop to the insane hours to which we were so easily becoming acclimated again. I wondered if my lack of sleep had cost me the edge in my exchange with the doctor. As I drove, I had a most extraordinary idea about how to show her how to die (like I knew!). After all, I was and am a writer, so I would write her a story explaining my take on death. Of course, I needed a few characters to do that. So I created three main ones, one patterned a bit after my own personality, one patterned somewhat after Cindy's, and one patterned after the cardiologist who had not let me see himself. His heart. His mind. His reason for the passion behind his interest in alternative medicine. He had instead afforded me a blank slate! I would use him and make him into anything the page demanded and let him help me teach Cindy how to die in peace. More than that, I resolved to write a little bit every day and call Cindy myself at an earlier, less ungodly hour, and read to her as I wrote.

When I arrived back home, I wrote the first 5000 words before dark. In fact, I wrote the beginning and the ending that first day. Very much like I have done with this memoir of sorts. I wrote the introduction and closing at the same time. All one has to do after that is fill the space in the middle. I never read Cindy the ending to what came to be titled "Malignant Emotion" until the entire story (minus the ending) had been shared, one day at a time, a few paragraphs per reading. Then I drove down and spent the weekend with her and read it aloud to her from beginning to end. We were sitting at a booth in the back of a nice steak restaurant when I finally read her the last few pages. We had been interrupted several times by former students who had spotted her and come over to say hello. They loved her, too! It was impossible not to be captivated by her unique and brilliant mind as well as her sweet mischievous zest for life! We had finished eating and the crowd was dwindling. It was almost closing time as I read her the last 20 or so pages. When I was finished, she reached across the table and took my hand and said, "Oh, Mary Jane, you died FOR me!"

"No," I said, "I died because it was the best way, I could think of to show you how someone else already did that nearly 2000 years ago. He's gotcha covered, kid!"

That project was supposed to be private and personal. Something special between just Cindy and me. But in her extraordinarily precocious and convincing way she made me promise, literally on her death bed, that I would publish it. She had gifted me a beautiful pen a few weeks after I had read the book to her in its entirety. It was engraved with the words "Novelist at Heart."

It was several years later when I finally kept my promise and published "Malignant Emotion." Malignant emotion was a term I actually thought I coined as I explored how negative emotions affect us physically, but in my research I learned that the Chinese had used the term for many long years, centuries actually, and they already knew the damage it can do.

After I published that book, a few readers responded with a request that I rewrite the ending and do a sequel. There were readers who quite simply had fallen in love with Vic, a lesser character if there are such people in any of our lives. They wanted me to write more about him. Maybe I will someday… That really might depend on how much more he reveals about himself as I write this bit of nonfiction. For some reason, as I try to write about my life, I think he is lurking patiently in the shadows waiting to be asked to come forward again. We shall see.

CHAPTER THREE

I suppose I always have aspired to be a healer. Even as Cindy was dying, I wanted to help heal her deepest hurts and anxieties. I remember a doctor who once told me I was sensitive to a fault. He said that I cared too much and tried too hard to make things better. He may have been correct. Maybe. Maybe not. I know, at one point, in my professional nursing years, as I assisted a physician in debriding a really angry dog bite wound, I realized that just soothing things over and applying antibiotics or a bandage truly was not always the way to go. Sometimes, you must go deep and clean out a wound and let it hurt and heal slowly from the inside out. The lady with the dog bite came in every day for us to do that for her, until eventually her leg healed.

That is what writing does for me. It heals me from the inside out. Right now, I am still reeling from deep grief following the death of my fifty-year life partner and I need to heal. So once more, I am looking back over my life in an effort to heal me. I had left nursing in 1986 to pursue writing and broadcasting although I did not know it at the time. I just wanted to write a newspaper column, then a few books, but way sure leads to way and paths unimagined often open to us. While my lifelong inquisitiveness had served me well when taking a patient's history, it served tremendously well when I made my career change at 38 years old.

Now I'm 72. It's 2020, the year of COVID-19 and racial unrest like none I've ever before personally witnessed. And, oh, how we all need healing!

It is important for me to try to understand what matters to me now in a world where we all want to matter in our efforts to encourage deep healing, inspire better understanding and build hope. I must, to some extent, incorporate story into my effort to do this because I think the study of scripture and especially the parables of Christ have taught me the importance of story-filled communication when I seek to better know and understand myself or another person.

So, who am I? What traits have made me into me? It is strange how my height immediately comes to mind as I think about my life. I have heard the "tall drink of water" and "I bet you enjoy being tall, you can reach everything" and "my goodness, you sure do carry yourself well to be so tall" comments. And there are the other comments, usually in reference to long legs which I suppose are a feeble attempt at flattery. Now. But not when I was in 7th grade and found myself towering over all the guys who seemed intimidated at the idea of even standing next to me. When those hormones are shifting and you are feeling your first drawing to the opposite sex, there is nothing fun about being taller than every boy in sight! I like how in recent years the film industry has incorporated that height issue into first dances and first kisses. I smile when I see a girl dancing with a boy six inches shorter. Yep, I do, but that was not me.

That was not me for many reasons. One, dancing was not allowed in my home. I know many Christians who appear to be very comfortable with their early introduction to faith and who have a long abiding love for Christ. I do not belong in that mix. I first asked Christ to come into my heart at age eight because I had heard a terrifying sermon about hell! For many years, as I heard various preachers talk about the concept of being "saved" and "experiencing salvation," I wasn't sure that eight-year-old's prayer had been heard. Then when I was 16, I heard a sermon entitled "God is Love." I really liked that love sermon and I wanted to get baptized and openly profess my faith after hearing such beautiful words. The sermon diffused a lot of the guilt and condemnation which had always seemed to be the focus in the churches of my youth.

Of course, there was the good stuff, too - the community fellowship, shared meals, singing and testimony (storytelling!) time, and occasionally what I came to perceive as true worship. At any rate, dancing, playing cards, going to movies, wearing shorts or pants, and other things were not allowed in my family. All of which continued to shore up a need within me to perform right and well. To behave and be good. And to suffer horrible feelings of guilt when I failed.

Being three months pregnant when I married set me up for the ultimate sin and guilt trip. So, at age 23 I decided to get baptized again and try to wash it all away. That didn't work. It took an in depth nine-month bible study into the Fourth Gospel, the Book of John, to set me free. We studied all the Gospels, but the emphasis was on John's and for the most part we used Kay Arthur's Precept Upon Precept study materials. After my exposure to that kind of bible study everything changed. In October of that year, at age 30, I asked Jesus to be my best friend. I wonder now if He knew what that ride would entail, but here we are, 52 years later and Jesus remains my absolute best buddy!

CHAPTER FOUR

In looking back at how I became me, there was something else in my early church exposure that shaped my life. Two things. One, singing around the piano after church, after going home with friends or having friends into our home. Singing during church services not so much, but those gatherings around the piano before and after, and in between church, helped mold me. Two, I had friends at church who played guitars and I often was invited to their home after church.

Once Sunday dinner (the noon meal of the south) was devoured and the dishes were done, we gathered on the front or back porch and they played and sang. Those times have a special niche in my memory bank. They are probably why I still enjoy and deeply appreciate so many aspects of traditional country music, especially the ways it can so simply tell a story, heavily drenched with emotion from all sides, often inspiring empathy where one would not always expect empathy to be inspired.

This is one reason I experienced such joy working editorially with Chuck Hancock on his memoir. He and I share a deep appreciation for how country music lyrics can paint such vividly memorable pictures. He recently reminded me it was not just porches, but in barns and under shade trees as well, where we gathered to enjoy the music of our youth. Regardless of genre, I think most would agree that music is powerfully influential in all our lives!

CHAPTER FIVE

Another observation as I look back at my life is that I seem to have preferred male friendship over female. I think, in my case, it is because I was so close to my dad growing up and was never really close to my mother. I loved my mother and I know she loved me, but I clearly was a daddy's girl and it marked me for life. Most men are so different from most women, often more direct, not so emotional. They are usually more ordered and focused. I, however, as my son said, am all over the place. A million or maybe just dozens of things are always going on in my mind. I love the way my guy friends can help me refocus, bring me back more quickly to the goal or goals at hand.

Truth be told, though, as I have aged, I have come to enjoy the ways some of my female friends can and will so readily explore our varied life experiences with no particular reason for doing so, just for the joy and fun of it or the simple healing therapy that it brings! At any rate, while I have liked men, now I find that I deeply appreciate female friendship as well.

We were in our second decade of marriage before my husband finally accepted my preference for male friendships. I was never sexually unfaithful to my husband (that would have meant more feelings of guilt!). I certainly was tempted a couple of times, once by none other than Tom Selleck. It was during what I look back as the only "bad" year of my marriage. Thus, I am thankful Tom and I only made lingering eye contact in the Florida airport that day as he was filming "Folks." I remember how the way he looked at me made me feel attractive, rare for me. When I look back at photos from my past, I think I was kind of pretty, but I sure did not think so through the years. Not at all.

While I valued my marriage as much or perhaps more than most women, I never put all my relationship eggs in one basket. That was something I never even entertained. Not at all. What I perceived to be God, or my desire to "know" God, came first. I came second and that meant interacting with a great variety of people and personalities through the years. All ages. Both sexes. Different races and nationalities. Diversity thrills me and that is a good thing because my husband and I were total opposites! He came third and because I put my own spiritual, physical, mental, and emotional health first, and always honored my personal interests apart from his (but not above his), I think I was able to love him quite well. In fact, I know I was.

I need to go back to my reference to never being allowed to dance growing up. There is another reason I would never have danced with guys shorter than me and trust me, they all were shorter! We were poor and there was no money for special event clothing or shoes tied to school activities. All extracurricular family and personal activities were tied to church where most other attendees also were poor. In fact, church was the only social constant in my life. We had moved 18 times by the time I was 18 years old. Daddy was always trying to find something a little more comfortable for our family of nine. Sometimes we had walls and floors without holes in them. Sometimes we had a bathroom. Always, we had family though, and church.

Church and faith are not necessarily connected for me. Church is more of a social institution. The growth of my faith has, in many respects, occurred in spite of church, but this is not the time or place to dwell on that. The truth is, in looking back at how poor we were, I am deeply thankful for the role of church attendance and the socializing (fellowship) that came with it.

Church socializing often meant good food. Dinners on the ground were my favorite. Fencing was stretched out over posts set in two rows about four feet apart in the church yard. My guess is that the specially constructed table was about 30 feet long. The wire fence atop those posts was stretched tight enough for tablecloths to cover it and food to be set out on it when we would have various food themed social events, especially homecomings. Those Homecoming Sundays, usually once a year, produced only the best efforts from everybody's kitchens. Real Southern cooking! Fried chicken. Baked ham. Potato salad. Beans, Peas. Creamed corn. Deviled eggs. Sweet Potato souffle. Oh my! Those annual spreads were something to be enjoyed.

So were the occasional fish fries when the bream (fish) were bedding (gathering to spawn and therefore easier to catch because they will hit just about any lure you throw at them). The men of the church took the initiative when it came to fish centered events. They caught them. They cleaned them. They fried them and the hushpuppies, too, of course. A good hushpuppy recipe is rural south gold! The women prepared side dishes. I loved those fish fries and sometimes there was swamp gravy as well. That was when the men would drain off all the grease and then add to the drippings that were left in the bottom of the pan just about anything one wanted to throw in! Potatoes, onions and tomatoes were almost always in the mix, along with some measure of hot sauce, but nothing was really off limits.

We all helped with the ice cream churning events (by hand, of course) with the little kids sitting on top of folded towels positioned on top of the churns to hold in the cold. Vanilla was always the crowd favorite, but I liked chocolate and banana and peach and strawberry. Still do! So, I'm not sure just when or how Italian food became my favorite food. Could be that spaghetti was the first thing I learned to cook as an adult. But well before I turned 30, I learned that there was a lot more to Italian cooking than spaghetti. Today, I so thoroughly enjoy the leisurely way I have learned to celebrate good bread, good olive oil, good wine, good company! Just about any truly Italian entrée out there will make me really happy now, but hold the garlic, please. Doesn't make sense does it, to hold the garlic on an Italian dish? Oh well, works best for me that way.

CHAPTER SIX

While my family had indeed moved 18 times before I left home, we always stayed within a fifty-mile radius of Albany, GA. There's something about the rural south, something special. It sticks to your ribs. Makes a survivor out of you. And for sure, I chose to be a survivor in the face of a number of life experiences that prompted me to consider suicide more than once. I'm not comfortable saying that. Not at all. But the truth will set you free they say, so let's go there. Claiming the freedom to be real, to be honest, and to be vulnerable might help move all of us toward healing.

My early childhood interaction with my paternal grandmother who practiced a few aspects of what I now consider witchcraft - all in the name of Jesus - set me up for some hard times, emotionally and spiritually. This started sometime between ages three and five, maybe even before. She worshipped me. Literally. Smothered me horribly. I am certain that also probably played a huge role in why I came to prefer male friendships over female. At any rate, many years later, in therapy, my psychologist diagnosed me with PTSD based on stories I shared about my grandmother.

Of course, she did not know the deeper cause when she first made that diagnosis because I did not talk about the rape that occurred when I was nineteen. I am not going into details in this writing either because my rapist is dead now. I don't think there's any need to accuse someone of something if they are not around to defend themself. Anyway, for many years I blamed myself for it. I still do, to some extent, and that may be the reason for many of the rather complex issues and insecurities I have had to work through over the years.

Oddly, if you know me, have ever known me, or if you ever get to know me, you probably will not perceive me as being or feeling insecure. Perhaps I have both my grandmother and my rapist to thank for the perception which I suspect I tend to project. By the time I turned 14, I was putting up walls, establishing barriers, shutting out my grandmother. It broke her heart. It saved my life. Then after the rape, I became most extraordinarily observant, a trait that has served me ever so well in absolutely every area of my life. Those two individuals taught me more than I ever wanted to know about how dangerous it is to trust people and circumstances which are not always what we initially perceive them to be.

Longing to grow my faith in God and hold on to my distrust of humanity has been a humdinger of a balancing act. It is hard. It fatigues one. It hurts.

Then there is the issue of unfairness. I am sure I share an awareness of that with many. In my case, it may be tied in part to my grandmother and to my father. I always felt like they loved me more… Nevertheless, a strong awareness of unfairness was always around when I was growing up. I still encounter it today. A zillion times I have heard. "Life isn't fair, get over it." Maybe not a zillion, but certainly thousands of times those words have rang out in my world.

So, let me try to address a few of the manifestations of what I have perceived to be unfairness during my early years. I suppose in all honesty I have come to believe now that Life truly is not fair and that, to some degree, I really must simply accept that fact. My evolving faith has taught me, however, that there is much I do not see, and cannot know, and therefore I do not have all the insight and wisdom necessary to make such a broad statement. Nevertheless, I always felt like my dad loved me more than he loved my other siblings during the first 14 or 15 years of my life, and I know my grandmother did.

If it is possible to worship another being, a human. I feel like my grandmother actually and visibly to everyone, worshipped me. It was awful. But … she believed in me, too, though, which was sort of empowering. She trusted me. She showed me off.

She taught me various scriptures early in life. Well before I started to school, I could recite the 23rd Psalm and other bible passages. She also would make me pray privately and aloud in her presence each time we would visit her. She repeatedly needed to hear me ask for forgiveness for all my sins so I could be in heaven with her someday. I still cringe when I recall those weird prayer times. I never got the feeling that it was about anything other than having me with her throughout eternity. I felt cornered. Smothered. It was during those forced prayer times that I learned how her dad made her do the same thing, and that it was he who taught her how to read coffee grounds, and see the past and future in other ways.

She tried to teach me how to tell fortunes, too, and "see" stuff I did not want to see or need to see. Then or now. Even then, I think I perceived much of her doings or teachings to be tied to the demonic, and I didn't even know about angels and demons and the spirit world like I do now. I just think the Holy Spirit protected me and gave me insight beyond my years.

She tried to keep me to herself and away from my cousins and other young people at her church all of whom I longed to play with when we visited her. I just wanted to be a kid, but I gave up on ever knowing a lighthearted playful childhood by the time I was seven or eight.

I think my dad probably followed her lead when he began to show me preferential treatment. There may be those who would enjoy that. I am not among them. The hurt and guilt that I felt for being loved the most is still painful even today. God and I have gone round and round about that many times.

That old Jacob and Esau story never set well with me. It did not seem fair when I first read it and still does not seem fair to me today. Beyond my own personal family life there were other things that did not set well with me as a young girl. Very early on, I would hear people whose skin was much darker than mine referred to as coloreds, niggers and hands. Hands were hired labor on the farms in our area. Those hands were usually blacks or African Americans as we tend to say today. Poor white folks who worked for the more well to do landowner were referred to as sharecroppers or sharecropper families. They often lived "free" on the boss man's land in exchange for helping plant and gather crops. The poor white sharecroppers seemed to be more respected than the colored or black workers were. Colored ladies often cleaned the homes of the white landowners and cared for their children. They cooked as well, but they could hold their own in the cotton fields, too.

My daddy had been in the Army Air Force during World War II and although he only had an eighth-grade education, he was able to get a job as a dispatcher at Southern Airways in Bainbridge, GA. When I was eight, he moved us away from rural living into Albany, GA where he took a job at Turner Air Force Base in Base Supply. In the afternoons, he did bad debt collections for a Loan Company to earn extra money. On Friday nights and all day on Saturdays he worked in small locally owned grocery stores as a butcher cutting up meat for customers. We ate well on Saturday night when he would get a good price on the unsold meat.

My favorite was the cubed beef steak he would bring home. It would be late, sometimes 10 p.m. or even later, but Mama would make mashed potatoes, open a can or two of early peas. We called them English peas. Often, we would have sliced tomatoes as well. That was culinary luxury! Still today, I enjoy that meal, but I prefer cubed wild venison over beef now. I think, as I write this, I am seeing for the first time a measure of white privilege in my own life in the sense that back then no black man would ever have been hired to cut the meat white folks bought and ate, or to collect bad debts. Just would not have happened.

CHAPTER SEVEN

Times were hard, but maybe, since we were white, times were not as hard as they could have been. We kids picked up pecans at nearby orchards to make extra money. We also picked grapes for my cousin who paid us by the bushel. It takes a lot of grapes to fill a bushel basket! One of my most painful memories is of a day when my mother paid a dollar for a broasted chicken. They were cooked out back behind a little country store not far from our house in East Albany. Back then you could buy a whole chicken for 30 or 40 cents, and when my daddy came home and discovered that Mama had paid more than twice that for just one chicken, he exploded. She cried. I actually went outside and got sick. It was just awful. I certainly did not want to eat any of that chicken after seeing the added misery it had brought into our home. I mostly just ate peanut butter and jelly sandwiches back then, before I developed an allergy to peanuts.

It actually was a food situation that led me to recognize one of the most unfair observations of my childhood. Near the meat market where my daddy worked on Friday night and Saturdays, there was a little hamburger joint next to an auto repair shop. This was back before I had ever heard of Krystal or White Castle burgers, but the burgers at this joint as we referred to it in that area of town, were small like theirs, very small and we could buy 10 for a dollar. For some reason, my daddy did not object, so we did that from time to time. That is where I first noticed the sign that said "Coloreds" with an arrow point to the sided of the building. I watched and coloreds always went to that window to place their order while whites ordered at the front. That was most extraordinarily odd to me. When I questioned it, I was told, "You don't eat or drink after coloreds."

Oh, mercy! There was something about the way my question was answered that suggested it would not be wise to ask why. So I didn't. Then. But I started watching. Looking. And sure enough, I began seeing signs at water fountains that said, "whites only." Sometimes I would see a fountain for "coloreds only" nearby, but sometimes I could not. I wondered where they drank water in public places. I wondered quietly though. Then around 1960 or 1961, a colored guy by the name of Martin Luther King made headlines in the local Albany paper. I read everything I could about him and his attempted movement towards equality concerning riding busses, ordering food, drinking water, etc. I told my daddy I thought we should march with him and help the coloreds get better, more fair treatment and access to goods and services.

I only said it once. My daddy loved me for sure and

he absolutely showed me a lot of favoritism, but trust me when I tell you his reaction to my questions assured me that I better never ask him THAT question again. To this day, I still do not understand his response. I hushed. I withdrew. I was 12 or 13 and had hit my growth spurt which meant I was towering over all the boys. Insecurity ruled and reigned in every fiber of my being. Questions churned within me, questions about religion and race and poverty and prejudice and fear and even politics.

President Eisenhower often came to the Albany area to hunt and that would make the paper, too. And though we definitely were poor, we somehow subscribed to Reader's Digest which I loved! One day my daddy bought a set of encyclopedias from a door to door salesman. Oh, happy day! With that set of encyclopedias came a Number One and Number Two Dictionary. In the back of the number two dictionary was a section called "Quotable Quotes." Heaven came down when I discovered it. Believable quotes from mostly dead people I had never heard of brought answers to some of my questions, addressed many of my deep wonderings, and seemed to assure me from beyond my time and circumstances that it was okay to wonder and to question.

Integration happened the year after I graduated. It

was not fun. My younger sisters were among a small group of whites who were bussed to the colored school. They were resented just as much, maybe more than the handful of colored children who were entered into the white schools. A couple of the guys "beat up" one of my sisters. There were meetings with parents at school. Turned out my mama knew their mama. When that mama heard what her sons had done, she "beat them." They did not bother my sister again.

Jumping forward to nursing school, I reckon I am going to have to be a little more vulnerable and honest than I would prefer in most situations. I made friends with two colored sisters who were in the class with me though I think we were already to starting to say black more often than colored at that point. I sure will be happy when we all stop referring to people by the color of their skin. Anyway, I worked part time on the weekend as a nurse's aide in the local hospital. My primary assignment was usually in the newborn nursery where I worked with two colored nurses who introduced me to black gospel. In the wee hours of the morning, I think it started at 5 a.m. when they would turn our department radio to a station that played nothing but black gospel until we got off duty at 7 a.m. It was auditory heaven! Not a soul in the churches of my youth had ever managed to make a sound like what came across those airwaves. That introduction to such a passionately soulful praise sound blessed me then and blesses me still.

I reckon it is time to spit it out, just go ahead and confess that during that period, for a great number of reasons I kind of was not into Jesus. If I felt anything toward him then it was jealousy. I tried to deny Him altogether but a gay friend of mine would not allow that. He argued with me and was always open to discussing the scriptures in depth. Trust me, we had lots of questions, he and I, as we embraced our differentness. I remember one day he asked me to promise him that I would just table those questions for the time being and not deny Christ just yet. He said, "After all, he truly was a historical being. You can decide later what you want to believe about him spiritually or religiously." That sounded like a plan, so I followed his suggestion.

Looking back, I think Jesus kind of liked it, too. I promise you I have never felt any true spiritual condemnation for all the questions I have asked and all the wonderings I have had. In fact, one day, when I was sixteen, I was sitting in the family station wagon alone outside our little country church waiting for "Training Union" to start at six. I think that is what we called the hour before actual worship. Anyway, I had my bible open to the first chapter of Isaiah and a butterfly with red and white dots on it flew in the window and landed on Isaiah 1:18. I could not believe it. I slammed my bible shut on it. I believe to this day that God sent that butterfly to tell me He would always talk with me and reason with me if I would be honest with Him. So yeah, my friend's suggestion that I table so many of my questions for later turned out to be a really good idea. Timing is everything. Scripture first told me that, but life sure has confirmed it.

Ok, so here is one part that I really do not want to share, but it may be important. You see, I have a gift of sorts, an ability I do not know how to explain (more about it later, maybe). It's a way of knowing things. I probably could commercialize it, if I had learned the tricks of my grandmother's trade, and it was a trade, people paid her to tell their fortune! I saw them pay her. Truth is, I probably would be good at it, but I have never wanted to use it for monetary gain. I am not alone in possessing this ability. My mother had it. And the author River Jordan has it and her mother. River's novels made me feel less weird. A little less alone. Less troubled. I remember talking to my mother when I was thirteen about some things I so easily "just knew." That is when she told me I was different. Her words frightened me. Made me feel lonely. To some degree, my mother had the same strange gift or ability, as well.

One day, when I came in from nursing school, Mother met me at the door and said, "Who was the black man you had lunch with?" It was not a discussion I wanted to have with her, so I did not have it. However, I had been at a regional event where nursing students and teachers from other schools were present. One of the school administrators, a nice black guy, considerably older than me, had joined me at my table over lunch. I was sitting alone for some reason, probably because I enjoyed it then and still do today. It affords me the opportunity to do more observing of people and eavesdropping on the conversations around me. I kept sensing during lunch that he wanted to ask me out, like on a date, but I'm glad he did not. I think I might have said yes and, in 1967, in Albany, GA, nothing safe could have come of us being seen together socially.

I am not uncomfortable talking about having lunch with a black guy in 1967. It is unnerving, however, that my mama "knew" as she washed dishes at the kitchen sink and "saw us" together. That is a hard gift to accept, to own, to know what to do with it. When we cannot understand or explain or prove something, it can be painful to speak of it.

I still have friends and relatives who resent interracial dating and marriage. I have those dear to me who also continue to refer to blacks as "niggers." I suppose if I am to be "fair" to those people, which is hard, I must say they also use the terms black and colored when they deem it appropriate, while reserving the term "nigger" primarily for those who they think are lazy or into crime. There are derogatory terms like "lazy ass hick or whore" and worse, that these same people use to describe white people who are irresponsible and won't work, or who have learned to "work" government assistance programs, sometimes quite fraudulently. I know that having white skin has afforded me a degree of benefits that those with darker skin have not had. I also know that in recent decades those with darker skin, which enables a claim of minority status, have been afforded opportunities that I and others with white skin in America have not had.

I have worked since I was 13. I like to work. I reckon that kind of brings me around to the way I tend to judge people, too. I primarily gravitate toward seeking more intimate friendship with folks who have a strong sense of empathy and a good work ethic. I do not like to be with people who lie, cheat, kill and talk incessantly although I know that they too have their story. Sometimes, I even want to hear it. Sometimes, but not always.

I am surprised at the roads of recall I appear to be heading down as I pen my memories. I think I want the journey though. Time will tell. One thing I love is the open road. I wonder if the wide-open fields and rural back roads of my youth planted that yearning in me. Road trips are something I enjoy alone or only in the company of someone who will not talk a lot.

I also enjoy good films, primarily dramas and comedies, and some television programming. I was a member of the drama club in high school. I now enjoy being able to crawl into a real or imagined character's mind as I write and become one with that character on the printed page. Maybe Vic does have a chance of getting his own story, his own book. We will see.

CHAPTER EIGHT

There are many other-worldly truths and realities in my life that are more reliable than most of the clocked or calendared events that time as we know it dictates. I now am choosing to discerningly turn back toward those things ... formerly unexplained dreams, visions, experiences, happenings. I am remembering and writing of some of them as I become the new me that death and grief requires. It will be what it was, and is, as I become what I will be during whatever tomorrows are left for me in this realm.

For more than 30 years, as a columnist, author, and broadcaster, I have helped thousands to have their stories told and heard. I will continue to enjoy doing that, but now I need to tell mine, too. When I was young, extrasensory perception (ESP) were the buzzwords for sort of supernaturally knowing stuff that others did not understand how you could know. I had it. I still have it. I thought everybody did until my mom told me when I was about 13 years old that they did not. As I said, that was hard to hear, but it helped me to better understand people I had started labeling quite inappropriately. I was wrong to do that.

Later, after leaving the nursing profession and entering journalism I would discover "Desiderata" by Max Ehrmann, which further helped me in my struggle to try to balance what I often knew so well, and others could not seem to know at all.

Go placidly amid the noise and haste and remember what peace there may be in silence. As far as possible, without surrender, be on good terms with all persons. Speak your truth quietly and clearly; and listen to others, even to the dull and the ignorant, they too have their story. Avoid loud and aggressive persons, they are vexations to the spirit. If you compare yourself with others, you may become vain and bitter; for always there will be greater and lesser persons than yourself. Enjoy your achievements as well as your plans. Keep interested in your own career, however humble; it is a real possession in the changing fortunes of time. Exercise caution in your business affairs, for the world is full of trickery. But let this not blind you to what virtue there is; many persons strive for high ideals, and everywhere life is full of heroism. Be yourself. Especially, do not feign affection. Neither be cynical about love, for in the face of all aridity and disenchantment it is perennial as the grass. Take kindly to the counsel of the years, gracefully surrendering the things of youth. Nurture strength of spirit to shield you in sudden misfortune. But do not distress yourself with dark imaginings. Many fears are born of fatigue and loneliness.

Beyond a wholesome discipline, be gentle with yourself. You are a child of the universe, no less than the trees and the stars; you have a right to be here. And whether or not it is clear to you, no doubt the universe is unfolding as it should. Therefore, be at peace with God, whatever you conceive Him to be, and whatever your labors and aspirations, in the noisy confusion of life, keep peace in your soul. With all its sham, drudgery and broken dreams, it is still a beautiful world. Be cheerful. Strive to be happy. - Max Ehrmann

I have learned to try to be discerning as I share insights that come out of the blue, like a silent whisper from somewhere or someone to my subconscious or conscious mind. In my early twenties I begged for that misunderstood and impossible-to-control ability to be gone. It was distracting and quite often there was nothing I could do to change anything about the disturbing circumstances I would be shown in advance of their happening.

Occasionally those revelations would come in a dream, while sleeping, like when I was 17 and dreamed of the US Embassy in Cairo, Egypt being on fire. Another vivid time was on July 17, 1996, when TWA Flight 800 went down. And no, folks, it was not sudden death in the air. It was agony for many on board. Not everybody died quickly. More often my knowing would happen like it did that day, while I would be wide awake and totally unable to respond. Helpless.

I know you want examples so I will share a few. One day, when I was a young mother, I started down the steps of our back deck and suddenly I saw a vision of the top of my son's head and I knew he was hurt. I turned back and went to the kitchen and stood by the phone, certain it would ring momentarily. It did. My son had cut his head while playing on the monkey bars at school.

Of course, the first time I ever remember sharing my ESP ability publicly and quite matter-of-factly was at my grandmother's house on a Sunday afternoon. I was not a teenager yet, and I had just started participating in "Sword Drills' at our church where a moderator would call out the location of a bible passage and the first to find it would step forward and read it. I do not think of myself as overly competitive, but I did like performing well in those Sword Drills. Of course, back then I had no idea how learning those passages would later impact my life – even save my life. More about that later. So, we were visiting my grandmother and the plan was to leave her home and drive straight to church that Sunday evening. I approached my dad around mid-afternoon and asked if we could please leave early. He asked why. I told him that we were going to have a flat tire and I did not want to be late for my competition. He laughed. I begged. He walked out to the car with me and showed me that all the tires were good and there was no need to worry. I persisted. He finally agreed to leave a little earlier than planned. We had a flat. I knew we would. We were a few minutes late for church, but we did arrive before the competition started. I was glad.

In my late twenties I worked part time for a doctor who went through a pretty nasty divorce and money became a problem, so he started writing illegal prescriptions for a couple of popular street drugs back then. A friend peddled them, and they split the money. I did not know about it at the time, but I had a series of three dreams about him that prompted me to warn him of coming dark times. The dreams made no sense to me. Later, months later, I dreamed of his father's death. It was another of what I have come to perceive as prophetic dreams. I saw his dad in the hospital bed. I saw the room. Vividly. I saw his dying. Again, I felt compelled to go share my dream with my doctor friend. The rumors had begun, and I was no longer working for him by then. This time, he listened. He knew there was no way I could know about the scene I described so now that I had his attention, I reminded him of the other dreams. Later, years later, after his arrest, conviction and upon being released from prison, he came to my home, sat on the chair in my kitchen under the yellow wall phone (I remember it so vividly) while I made chili, and he thanked me for trying. Nobody else had even tried to sway him from the crimes that sent him to prison, he said. Of course, it was hard to take credit because I knew that I had done it reluctantly and primarily to avoid discomfort. While there have been many times when I could do nothing about my insights and revelations, when I could or can, I felt and feel miserable if I did and do not. I suppose I often have acted on the supernatural leads more out of selfishness than a desire to truly serve my fellow man. I just do not like to feel guilty about not doing something when there actually is something I can do, and I wrote the following poem in reference to this fact.

i do not know any better
than to just go barging into peoples' lives
when they're hurting 'cause i've been there
and i've wondered if somebody cared
so when i care i try to show it ... or how will they know it?
oh, sure!
i know there's always prayer
and i could just pray that God would meet the need
and heed the cry of each aching heart
and do His part to make it all better
and i could ask Him to send somebody
to feed, clothe, comfort, encourage
but then there was that time i asked Him
to do just that for them
and He said to me
"you are SOMEBODY"

The truth is I do know better. I just must do what I must do in order to keep the peace. MY peace. My personal sense of wellbeing that comes when I act in one of those moments that matters on behalf of others. I do like to make a positive difference in the lives of others whenever I can, but trust me, most of my actions that are often misunderstood by others take place because I want to preserve my own peace of mind.

Like one time, probably around 2008, not sure of the date, I was driving to Nashville for a convention and I stopped at a Cracker Barrell just north of Chattanooga. It was noon, and the place was packed. I was seated against the wall adjacent to the gift area and was waiting for my lunch to come. About the time the server set it down in front of me, I glanced up to see two ladies walk into the dining area. The greeter seated them at the table in front of the fireplace where the checker-board game is most often displayed. As they entered, I had an ESP flash. It said, "Go touch her and pray for her."

"Oh, heck no," I muttered silently to the Source of the instructions.

It came more loudly, definitely not a soft whisper this time, "Go."

"No, just no!"

"Go."

"No."

I glanced down at my food. Appetite fading. Angry. Strange how anger motivates me. Even now, while I write this memoir, anger is in part a catalyst that has me finally putting words on paper. So, I stood up, in anger, to just leave because I could no longer eat, but my feet would not walk out in the right direction. I literally went straight to the older woman and bent to ask very softly if I could please touch her arm and pray silently for her.

Oh, my! She grabbed MY arm and exclaimed, "NO!

Pray aloud." At that point, a stare or two got leveled in our direction. I turned behind me and asked if I could take a chair from a neighboring table. Thankfully, those patrons said yes. I pulled it over to where the two ladies were sitting, plopped down so I would not be so conspicuous and softly said, "No, I will pray silently." I'm 5'8' tall. I can be a spectacle. I did not want to be seen or heard.

Oh, well! As soon as I touched the older of the two ladies, I had this awareness of her being very distraught about a conversation she must have soon and I simply prayed that God would give her the words to say. That was it. When I opened my eyes, she clutched my hands and begged, "Please, please tell me what you prayed."

Aiyiyi! So very softly I whispered the essence of my super short prayer to her.

She cried out to her daughter to go get a camera out of the car and take a picture of the angel God had sent to minister to her on the worst day of her life. Then she told me she had just left her doctor's office and he had told her she had less than three months to live. She and her daughter had stopped by Cracker Barrell to have a glass of iced tea before going home to tell her granddaughter, who was the joy of this grandmother's life, that death would soon come.

The daughter went to the car and got the camera, returned, and took our picture. I never knew their names. I left the restaurant. My untouched food was still on my table. I do not think I told her how much God loved her. I wish now I had taken time to hear more of her story. One thing is for certain she was a real big deal to her Heavenly Father. Probably still is. Shucks, she may even be peeking over my shoulder now as I tell you about her. I think I would like that.

Then there was another time back when I was still a nurse (I've had a lot of identities and I still love 'em all). I was working for a family practitioner. We were not taking any new patients at the time and as I approached the front desk to pick up a chart and call a patient back to an exam room, a strange man walked up to the window and asked the receptionist if he could be seen. She asked if he was already a registered, established patient and he said no. She told him she was sorry that we were not accepting new patients at the time. It happened as I greeted my patient and led her to an examining room.

"Go get him," were my instructions from my inner voice that I imagine nobody else can hear.

"Seriously?"

"Yes, seriously."

I turned back quickly and laid down the chart on the front counter and raced out through the waiting room into the parking lot yelling, "Hey, mister!"

He turned around and said, "Me? You mean me?"

"Yes, you. Come back. The doctor will see you."

Of course, I did not know how I was going to make that happen, but I knew it HAD to happen. In those few short minutes, I "knew" the man's very life depended on it.

Many months later, after the man had survived the stomach cancer that was discovered through tests that were done following his first visit at our office that day, after his health was restored, after he had gone back to building houses, after all that and more … he told me that he had planned to end his life that fateful afternoon if the doctor had refused to see him. Two other doctors had failed to find anything wrong with him and he knew something was terribly wrong.

I can tell many stories of how my ESP has influenced my life and the lives of others and I may share more later in this book if any of those stories ask to be told, but for now I only will share enough to help you better understand what happened the night I met JesseLee.

CHAPTER NINE

First, you already know that I like music - all genres to some extent, mainly because I so appreciate the creative process. I enjoy blues, jazz, most of the big band era sounds, and black gospel, Americana as well, some Contemporary Christian songs, but my personal favorite is the old traditional country followed by Christian Country because of their easy and honest simplicity in sound and lyrics as well as the way they tell great stories. Therefore, I've long appreciated Nashville, TN, the Home of the Grand Ole Opry and Traditional Country Music. In a literary sense, however, I was first drawn to Music City in 2003, to research the town when I was penning a project that would later become my novel entitled "Malignant Emotion." I created a fictitious character in that novel whose life was, to some extent, tremendously influenced by Lower Broadway in Nashville. I adored my special character, Vic, as did many readers, who requested a sequel and asked that I further develop his story. I entertained the idea for a while, then life got in the way. Like I already said, maybe Vic is still waiting for me to better understand his rather unique journey. I hope so.

Anyway, it was more than a decade later, in November 2014, when I met JesseLee, seven years after I had discovered "Inspirational Country

Music." Back in 2007, somebody had told me that Inspirational Country was the fastest growing genre in America. I did not believe it. So, that year, I had driven to Nashville to research the claim. Vivian Perry had invited me to an ICM convention at Trinity Music City, near Hendersonville, TN. I met three men that week who would prove to be tremendous influences in my life in the years ahead. They were Tommy Brandt, Greg McDougal and Jayc Harold. Later, I would meet and work with many others including Chuck Hancock, Daniel Cowart, Leo Johnston, Aubree Bullock, Mary James, Hunter Logan, Erik Grant Bennett, Taylon Hope and so many other extraordinarily gifted recording artists who may later show up on these pages or in works to come, especially Peter MacDougall, whose song, "Broad Road," influenced my title for this book.

It was at that first convention where I walked by an open door to a backstage dressing room and overheard Tommy Brandt say to Greg McDougal and Ricky Skaggs, "I feel like God is leading me to Georgia, but I don't know anyone in Georgia."

I stopped, stepped back, stuck my head in, and said "I'm from Georgia. You can come get to know me."

Two weeks later, his wife, Michelle, called and asked if I was serious about my invitation. I said yes. They came and stayed for two weeks. That was the beginning of an eternally enduring relationship! A few years later, in 2011, Tommy was traveling through, stopped to visit, and while parked at our farm in his tour bus, he experienced several cancellations that resulted in a glorious six-week visit. He helped me set up my recording studio when a broadcasting career, which I never sought, was handed to me. More about that later. Maybe.

Back to 2007. After I arrived on scene at that first Inspirational Country Music event, I got into a conversation with Jayc which led to me asking him if we could leave the convention center and go find a quiet coffee shop somewhere so I could listen better. Jayc is not a big talker so I'm not sure what happened that day, but we found a coffee shop and I listened as he talked long about moving to the United States from Canada, about his beloved wife and family, but mostly about his mom. He was grieving over losing her and his grief still was fresh. It was an honor to listen to him that day. When we returned to the convention setting, I learned that folks were about to put an APB out for him. Yep, we had disappeared.

For now, I mention Jayc to say that seven years later, in 2014, when I returned to Nashville to cover that same annual convention, as I walked into the back room of the Nashville Palace (referred to at the time as the "Parlor'), Jayc and his Honky Tonk Opry team were on stage performing. They were the opening act for the week. And literally, as I walked into the room, a man I had never seen or heard stepped up to the microphone and started to sing.

That is when it happened.

I was in mid step and I heard my little voice clearly say, "Help him."

I instantly knew to whom the voice in my spirit was referring.

I argued silently, "You have to be kidding. THAT guy assuredly does not need my help."

"Help him," came the voice once again.

"Ugh!" I groaned in my spirit.

I had just finished interviewing a most delightful physician, Dr. Sally Burbank, who had written a book we both had enjoyed talking about, "Patients I Will Never Forget." I was prepared to sit down and just enjoy myself for the evening.

I already told you that I have always loved traditional country music, but in recent years I had come to really enjoy inspirational country, so much so that I hosted "Corner of Country with MJ", for three years before launching my REACH to

TOUCH talk show. And Jayc Harold's most unique honkytonk gospel sound is meant to be casually enjoyed to the fullest.

But my peace had been messed with, and I must force myself to respond when that happens, so I looked around for the man who was coordinating the week's events and asked him about the guy singing on stage with Jayc's band.

"That's JesseLee," he said. "He owns this place."

I learned later that he did not actually own the Nashville Palace, but he was the proprietor at the time. I discovered that he had a two-year contract with the family who did own it, and everybody was hoping that JesseLee's fame down on Lower Broadway in Nashville would help bring the Palace back to life. JesseLee was the owner of Robert's Western World and a staunch defender of traditional country music!

I got myself introduced to the lady who was managing the Palace for JesseLee and asked her if I could briefly meet him. I specifically asked for a fifteen-minute interview. She said no that he was too busy, had a big week ahead of him, and he was trying to get out of there early.

I said ok and started to settle back and just enjoy the music all the while kind of gloating and telling my inner voice, "Well, I tried!"

Then came the tap on my shoulder. I turned to hear the bar manager say, "Jesse says he will give you five minutes."

Oh, my! My gloating abruptly ended.

I stood up and walked with her to an almost unbelievably cluttered and crowded office where three women were working on various things, and the music from concerts in both the front and the back of the Palace were vibrating through the walls. I could barely hear myself think or speak. To hear him talk, and record our conversation, would be quite the challenge, so he said, "Let's go in a closet." That worked fairly well, and I kept things short although I do think I actually got my requested fifteen minutes. But when I turned off the microphone, there in that closet, the real conversation began.

JesseLee started to pour out his heart to me. My own heart began to break for him. It still breaks for him today. An hour or so later when we came out of the closet, I attempted to leave as a couple of the women in the room shot daggers in my direction. JesseLee insisted, however, that I sit down in front of a computer and listen to something. It was a recording of him singing "Something About That Name" written by Bill and Gloria Gaither. I listened quietly and tearfully. We both had been crying in the closet and the flow of tears remained at ready. Then I thanked him and started once more to exit. He said no, wait, and played it again. Then he played it a third time before he finally seemed willing to let me slip out, but not before he gave me several copies of his "Learning To Lean" gospel CD and told me that if he survived the surgery that was scheduled for that following Tuesday and could get well, then he wanted to dedicate the rest of his life to singing music that would "glorify Heavenly Father." Before I finally left the room, he asked me to come to his house and see him before I left town. He expected to be back home by Thursday of that week.

I left his office crying.

I cried all night and all the next day. I was a spectacle. Numerous concerned artist friends asked what was wrong. I truly could not understand the impact my exchange with JesseLee had on me. I still do not fully understand, but I do know that there were angels in the midst as demons danced on the broad ways of many lives the night of our first encounter. I also know that those moments spent in what became my first literal prayer closet mattered. I think Jesus was onto something when he recommended closet prayer. A special group intercessory time was scheduled for JesseLee that week, and several men of great faith approached God's throne on his behalf.

I had told a number of the artists that I would be following up and checking on JesseLee before I left town. Many of them gave me copies of their latest CDs to share with him. I had a couple of my earlier books in the car, and while walking through Cracker Barrell around the corner from the Nashville Palace, there on Music Valley Drive, I spotted a huge display bear (really big!) and talked the manager into selling it to me. He said okay because they were about to change out that display anyway.

On Thursday I drove to JesseLee's home with all the gifts in hand. A friend of his took the CDs and books and put them in a closet. JesseLee hugged the bear. He said he had never had one. The bear was almost as big as him. I visited briefly, had prayer, then left. A few days after returning home I called the manager at the Palace to ask about him. About two weeks later, she suggested that I call him directly because she thought he was up to a phone conversation at that point.

I called.

He thanked me again for the bear.

I told him about all the people who were praying for

him and asked him if he had enjoyed the CDs and books. He said he knew nothing about them. He could not remember them and said he had no idea what had happened to them. A couple of hours later he called me back to thank me for those gifts and said he had found them put away in a closet.

A few days later when we were chatting, after he had read parts of one of my books, he asked if I would write his life story. I was taken aback. Very taken aback. Of course, I would not understand my strong reluctance until much later. Those demons dancing on Broadway were mounting their attack and I did not have a clue. Not then. Jesse told me that another woman had attempted to write his story for him, but she had died in the process. Then he told me he had paid another woman $17,000 to write it, but she had quit in the middle of the project. All the time he was talking, I could hear the little voice from a few weeks earlier saying, "Help him."

I did not immediately say yes, however. I am a strong-willed, opinionated person who is not one bit reluctant to change my mind in midstream if I feel the need to do so. What people say or think quit mattering to me back in the late 1980's. Also, I almost always can make very quick in-the-moment decisions because not only do I usually gather a lot of facts before making major decisions, I also have my ESP. I do ok for the most part, but that day I said something I do not commonly say. Prior to giving him an answer, I said, "I will have to pray about this first before I can say if I will write your book."

"Ok, please do that first then," he said.

I called him back a couple of days later and said yes.

He asked, "What do you want me to pay you?

I said, "I want you to pay with your life."

You see, I truly had prayed and finally I understood all my tears the week I had met Jesse. God had given me a glimpse into his life and heart, and into his horrific suffering at the time. It was almost more than I could bear. I knew when I prayed about writing his book that it was close to being more than he could bear as well. I told JesseLee that my prayer had revealed to me the depth of his chronic pain and depression, along with how he was not wanting to live and the only way I would write his book is if he agreed to choose life.

"But I can pay you," he said.

"Then pay me by choosing life."

"But I am very sick," he said, "and if I die will you

publish my story?"

"Yes, I will," I said, "if you die from natural causes, but you must simply choose life if we are to work together."

That was late December. Following many long days and hours of indepth recorded interviews, I had the book written by the end of April. Then, along with an editor I hired in Georgia and two of Jesse's good friends in Nashville we began a series of what would become 13 editorial proof readings, four of them aloud. There were some accounts I had recorded almost exactly as he had expressed them, but he wanted me to soften some of the passages so as not to hurt others needlessly. Other pieces of his story also got edited out for various reasons.

Besides asking that JesseLee choose life, as we started working together, I also told him I expected to hear the truth as honestly as he himself could tell it, and that while not everything could be recorded in 100,000 words or less, I needed to hear his truth in full context so I could figure out the most efficient way to tell his story. He promised me truth. I know now that he did not share all of his truth with me. He could not. Very few of us can do that. It can hurt too much - us, and others - but I also know he did not lie. What he told me is what he believed to be the truth, measured truth, but truth, nevertheless. Of that I am certain. It was his memory and his reality at the time. Just like what I am sharing now about my own life.

It was a magnificent period of real heart to heart exchange, the kind any writer treasures. At one point as he talked at length about the three major past loves of his life, Jesse lingered long while speaking of Sybele, his first sweetheart back in Brazil, and told me she lived in Nashville now, and that I should meet her. He said her story was even more interesting than his and that he wished I would help her write it. Since JesseLee made that suggestion I have discovered that Sybele clearly does not need anybody's help in the telling of her story. She is a phenomenal writer, and many times has been a well-spoken guest on national television and radio talk shows in reference to her journey as a legal immigrant.

Both JesseLee and Sybele speak several languages. JesseLee wanted his story told in English, not Portuguese or Spanish or Italian and he is quite adept at jumping from one language to another in both word and song. He actually enjoys doing that, but he wanted his story in English so I chose to write it in first person to allow the reader a true glimpse of the heart of an extraordinarily gifted, but troubled young man who came to America with a dream that would not die. Sybele truly is a phenomenal writer and I am honored that she lets me share as a friend in both the living and the telling of her story which I hope will one day be in print. She lives just a few miles from me now in Georgia and has become a family member in every respect that matters. She recently, as a proud legal immigrant patriot, was instrumental in starting a movement called FREEDOM RIGHTS. Trust me, she needs no one to help her adequately express herself!

CHAPTER TEN

I had no idea how much my life would get turned upside down and inside out after I met JesseLee. He has said that the writing of the book was extraordinarily therapeutic for him. In looking back, I suppose I know now that it was for me as well. I do not know why the first woman died while writing his story. I do not know why the second woman walked away. However, I heard many things that could have had a bearing on those incomplete efforts. You see, there were aspects of JesseLee's story that many people would not believe. Some of which were included in "BRAZILBILLY, The JesseLee Jones Story." Some were not.

I share the copyright ownership of this work with JesseLee. I was going to sign it all over to him as a gift, but he refused it. He said he wanted to share ownership with me because I had, after all, written the book. I don't know, but I'm assuming it may have been in part because of health reasons, but JesseLee opted not to pursue the American marketing plan we had agreed upon for the book. Instead, he chose to publish an adaptation of the book in Portuguese for distribution in Brazil. That is where he chose to put his time and money, so I never profited from sales in America. Since we did not have a work for hire agreement and I never charged him for any of my work, I have the freedom under US copyright law to republish the book as well, under another ISBN, since we both co own the copyrighted material. Perhaps I will eventually do that. In fact, I would love to write a screenplay and see the book adapted to film.

I believed JesseLee because of my own exposure since early childhood to the spirit world which many either cannot see or simply refuse to see. I'm not sure which it is. So I know, firsthand, about angels and demons and wandering, manipulative spirits. I know much more than I understand, but I do know. Thus, hearing of Jesse's tormented childhood, and believing his memories, was not a stretch for me. I already knew too well about angels in the midst of the demons dancing on the many broad ways of all our lives, but I was about to learn so much more. No quality time spent working with any one person has ever revealed more to me about the spirit world than those many 2015 moments that mattered so much – those discerning moments, hours, days which I spent with JesseLee Jones.

In the telling of his story, JesseLee mentioned how Pastor Ron Blakely came to him not too long after he, JesseLee, had bought Robert's Western World from Robert Moore and asked Jesse if he could do a gospel show on Sunday mornings at the already world famous traditional country music honktytonk.

Jesse told him yes back then, and told me in 2015 that he believes that is why God has allowed him to be so profitable in his business – because he invited God into that bar which would come to be called the HonkyTonk Church of Lower Broadway.

When Jesse first started letting Pastor Ron use the bar for a Sunday morning worship time, he was young and a new business owner and still very much a worker bee. After the bar closed in the wee hours of the morning he would sometimes sleep for a while on the floor and then rise early to clean up for Pastor Ron Blakely to come in and sing gospel. Pastor Ron was a Godsend and from day one he has been thankful for the opportunity to minister boldly on Lower Broadway in Nashville, TN. I have sat in on that Sunday morning worship service several times while Pastor Ron on some occasions, and Jayc Harold at other times, have sung deeply worshipful gospel music.

It has been clearly demonstrated to me time and time again that the sweet Holy Spirit will go anywhere It is invited. Although I have never heard JesseLee sing gospel at Robert's, I have been told that he does occasionally do that. One lady told me how when he sings "There's a sweet, sweet spirit in this place…' a hush always falls over the crowd.

I often find it strange when I am in Nashville and

choose to pay a bloody fortune to park on a deserted Sunday morning, and walk several blocks through the stench of the drugs, booze and sex from the night before, to attend that old HonkyTonk Church. Its back door opens out into an alley where stands the Ryman Auditorium, once the Mother Church of Nashville. The effort on my part makes it easy to understand how Johnny Cash's song, "Sunday Morning Coming Down" still rolls so easily off the tongues of many Nashville singers. At Robert's Western World, I have been blessed to watch a simple, but genuine brand of worship among lingering drunks and ladies of the night, along with a scattering of tourists and a few regulars who call that old bar their church home.

CHAPTER ELEVEN

Perhaps this is as good a time as any to let you know there is no chronological outline to my ramblings in this memoir of sorts. I am just being me. Talking. Remembering. Wandering in print about some of the moments that have mattered so much in many circumstances of my life. Deciphering and sharing what I can with you. Freely. Literally letting my words fall wherever they want to fall in the order they choose. I am realizing as my words present themselves that I cannot share all I might like to share because of the way my sharing might affect others. I'm trying not to hurt others while I attempt to share openly and as honestly as I can about some of my interaction with the spirit world.

I believe there is God. I think I came from God and I think I will return to God, AND I think that whole trip to earth and return to heaven revolves around Jesus making a way for it to happen. That is what I believe. I quit trying to put "God" in a box when I was a kid and I have never allowed anybody else to try to put God in a box for me. In fact, one of my favorite poems (that I personally wrote) is about folks who once tried to label me and put me in a box. Didn't let that happen either!

> They boxed me up and labeled me
> And carefully filed me away
> A neatly packaged entity
> To probe another day
> I squirmed and fought
> And wiggled free
> My anxious thoughts fast fading
> For what they thought of me today
> Is not worth contemplating.

It was an attempt to label me with "Lupus" and an assortment of other medical diagnoses that inspired that poem. I think this is as good a time as any to tell you about Dr. Thomas Humber. For several reasons there would be no ink on these pages if it were not for him. I may be publishing a book later entitled "Dear Doctor, I am your teacher…," and in that work there will be more about my physical health and medical journey. Since I'm talking about so much that happened in 2007, however, Dr. Humber must get honorable mention!

First, you should know that I tend to compartmentalize my health issues. I very seldom allow thoughts about my physical body to interfere with thoughts about my life. I am not my body. My life existed before it ever got a body, and it will exist when this earth body finally wears out. That said, my physical body was suffering tremendously in 2006 and I saw my gastroenterologist on the day after Christmas that year. He had followed me before and after the removal of my colon in 2002. I had lots of issues. At that visit, I was horribly distorted with back and abdominal pain. As we discussed how to address it, that wise doctor said, "I think my wife might divorce me if she knew how you are suffering and learned that I did not refer you to her chiropractor."

Later that same evening, I had a chance encounter with an administrator I knew well from a large cardiology office. She just happened to be that same chiropractor's mother-in-law. She pulled out a card and said, "See Thomas. See him tomorrow." That was my "second witness." I knew hope was around the corner.

Thomas Humber saved my life. He also became a dear friend and prayer partner. His practices "atlas orthogonal" chiropractic as did his dad before him, and his nephew, Travis, after him, along with several other highly qualified practitioners at Atlas Chiropractic, just south of Atlanta, GA. In every respect my health improved under his care. I am so glad I never got into that box full of medical diagnosis labels.

While I am telling you how effective chiropractic is I think I need to mention a guy named Russ Foley, too. To be more specific, Russell A. Foley, MS, PT.

Russ, a world-renowned pain specialist, was the first physical therapist I ever saw for help with pain issues. It was back in 1988. He and his healing hands were a firm reminder that there's good reasoning as to why Jesus chose to be hands on instead of just speaking healing into the sick. Physical therapists and massage therapists have a rightful and important place in the healing practices!

CHAPTER TWELVE

God gave me a real strong streak of curiosity about much in this world, as well as an extraordinary ability to be motivated by anger. I have not always understood how those two traits can so consistently work both in my favor and on behalf of many others, but I have discovered that they often work in and through me hand in hand. Curiosity and anger. It is an interesting mix.

Just like I fought being labeled and somewhat angrily refused to be put in a box, I don't feel that God can be boxed up and presented in a package of any sort and certainly not a neat one! I hope God is okay with all the contemplation I have done about Him through the years. Yep, I see God as masculine. Very. You are welcome to do your own contemplating and have your own thoughts, but I reckon we all must wait to have our theories or conclusions confirmed at a later date. I do believe in judgment. Many of my fellow Christ centered believers do not seem to. Some, however, absolutely buy into a grand judgment day followed by the whole hell fire and brimstone eternal damnation kind of punishment, with those who have been saved by the atoning blood of Christ spending eternity back in Heaven with our Heavenly Father (God!).

I promised to be honest in the writing of this book and the truth is I just do not know what I believe about all that. I do know that my own story (life) is but a droplet from the breath of God blown out onto the winds of eternity. I also know that I know so little, but I will try to tell you what I am certain of as I go along... and that just ain't much.

I know that I grew up under the manipulatively smothering influence of a grandmother who I know, in looking back, was mentally ill, and with good cause. I was the first born to her baby son and his wife. She had four living children at the time of my birth and three dead ones. Two died shortly after birth. One girl, who clearly was her greatest pride and joy, died at around four years old if I recall correctly. Her husband, my paternal grandfather was a womanizer who delighted in molestation. He never touched me inappropriately, but I cannot say that about others I love and cherish. I am certain my grandmother would have killed him if he had ever molested me and she knew about it. Such was her obsessive devotion to me from birth. My parents were living with these two grandparents when I was born and from the beginning my grandmother possessively referred to me as her "heart."

I mentioned earlier how much I enjoyed Bible Drills as a young girl. To this grandmother's credit it was she who first introduced me to the joy of memorizing Bible verses. I already told you how she had me learning the Twenty Third Psalm and numerous other passages before I could ever read and she took great pride in having me recite what she taught me before her church congregation. For that introduction to the Scriptures I am deeply thankful. For the other ways that she introduced me to the "power" of God's Word I still am disgusted and disheartened. To my angels who worked overtime back then and to the God who sent them to protect me, I say, "thank you."

Someone I love dearly who suffers from depression told me recently that the most hurtful thing for her is pondering "what might have been." I get that, but it does not depress me or even stress me anymore because life just is what it is and while the Bible may be our best play book, the fact (of this I am certain) is that it is often misused and abused. My grandmother did that, and she tried to teach me to do the same thing.

As she told those fortunes, she read coffee grounds, shared her prophetic dreams and tied her Bible up with string through an old-fashioned skeleton key tucked in the center of its pages. Then she talked to that bible. Sure did. She had me, as a young girl, place my finger under the fat part of one side of the key and she put her finger under the other side. Then she would ask questions of the bible and request that it "turn Bible key and all" to the left or right to say yes or no or respond when she called out certain names or places, etc. I think it worked very much like I am told a Ouija board works. I have never used a Ouija board and have no desire to do so. That Key-in-the-Bible thing was my first conscious introduction to trying to communicate directly with the unseen spirit world. It was real and I know now that angels were dancing passionately among the demons along the paths I first walked in this life.

Thankfully, I was born doubting. Questioning everything was first nature. My dad once offered me a nickel, when I was four, to please not ask "Why?" for just five minutes. I didn't take it. Heck, I would not stop asking questions for any amount of money. I think I already told you I like questions more than answers most days. Honest questions.

So, sure, I asked questions when my grandmother insisted that I play her bible, string, and key game. Very early on, I started trying to come up with questions that I could use to prove there was nothing to her trick. It got interesting. That thing we did together went on for about ten years, off and on. I learned much about the spirit world during that time. I suppose I am grateful for that exposure, at least to some degree. I know that it helped establish the basis for me to be able to believe JesseLee as he told me about his exposure to a dark spirit world as a young boy in Brazil.

Eventually, around age 14, I'd had enough. I could no longer stand the sight or smell of my grandmother. To have her attempt to hug me was almost unbearable. Such attempts on her part inspired my first horribly smothering claustrophobia attacks. I remained alienated as much as possible from her until I was 19 when she was dying and begged for me. I reluctantly drove to sit by her bedside all night, the night before she died. I later regretted going, but it was done.

A few years later, I was married, and my newborn son was in the crib in our master bedroom. My husband was at work (night shift) and we had a pistol in the drawer of the bedside table at the time. Our upstairs neighbor was a heavy drinker and when his wife (a flight attendant) was away he had attempted to break in on me a couple of times. A cop also lived in the building so somehow, we all managed without bloodshed. After all, the guy was golden when he was sober. Oh, well, I was still a good shot and that comforted me. When my hubby returned from Vietnam, he taught me to shoot a pistol, a rifle and a shotgun. Long story behind all that, but I needed to learn, so I did. Therefore, I was comfortable reaching for a pistol the night my dead grandmother showed up.

I know I am rambling, but you need that background as I tell you of how I was sleeping and heard the front door of our apartment open and close. I sat up in bed and reached for the pistol. I maneuvered over so if I shot whoever came through my bedroom door then the bullet would not go anywhere near my baby's crib. Then I heard her feet. Not my neighbor's. Hers. I sat there in the bed telling myself I had to still be asleep, that I must be dreaming, that there was no way her tiny dead feet could make their unique and quite memorable shuffling sound on the carpet like it did on the hardwood floors of her home. But that is the distinct sound I heard. Then when she turned in the hall to walk past by my bathroom door and into the bedroom, she spoke. It was only three or four sentences.

For a few weeks I remembered what she said, but I am so thankful that it eventually was erased from my memory. I don't know if I suppressed it or if I just begged God to take the words away and He did. I truly do not know. What I do know is that I never went back to sleep that night, and a couple of hours later after the streetlights turned to sunlight, and my hubby came home, I was still holding that gun. I'm fairly certain it would have been of no use to me against whatever spirit that was, but it gave me some degree of comfort, nevertheless. In the years since, I have entertained the idea of being hypnotized and having somebody help remember what she/it said, but the truth is I really do not want to know.

On very few occasions have I experienced an audible spirit. It happened at the Jekyll Island Club Hotel one time. That experience prompted me to delve deeply into the history of that place. Another time was one night, shortly after we moved to the wonderful farm where we lived for nearly 25 years. My son was sleeping in one of the upstairs bedrooms and my hubby was snoring horribly, so I went upstairs to sleep in the bedroom across the hall from my son. I turned on the overhead light, then walked over to turn on the bedside lamp before turning off the big light. I turned back the covers and in a somewhat sweeping motion as I started to lie down, I turned off the lamp. As I did so, the bedroom door opened and I heard a female voice say, "Here she is. I've found her. She's right here." I jumped up and turned back on the lamp. Nobody was there. I darted across the hall, wondering who in heck was sharing the bedroom with my son, but he was alone and sound asleep. I searched the whole house. There was no woman to be found. I went back to bed and went to sleep. What else could I do? Some questions don't get answered.

CHAPTER THIRTEEN

Some questions do get answered though. Sort of...
It was Saturday night, February 6, 1988 and my pregnant sister, Tamra, and I had left another sister, Lynda, at the hospital to continue the hideous death watch vigil we all were being forced to engage in while my dad lay dying. He had arrested (died) in the operating room earlier in the week, on a Wednesday, during his second open heart surgery, but the surgical team "miraculously brought him back" to die an inch at the time until his last breath was drawn on Sunday night, February 7th.

As I type these words, I realize I am still angry. I will always believe they needed him to be a Surgical Bypass or CABG "save." The surgeon and the hospital did not want that "death in the O.R." statistic. But those doctors knew my dad would not survive the week. I think they just wanted him to die on their terms, not his. He tried to die again around midnight on February 6th. There was another full arrest. That time, the CCU staff did their thing and brought him back.

The following morning, when Lynda called to tell me what had happened at the hospital, my questions about what had happened in our hotel room around midnight were answered. Tamra and I had gone to bed around 11 p.m., but she had been constantly up and down to urinate (early pregnancy does that!) and finally she was still again. I thought we were about to doze when I saw movement of a human shape at the foot of her bed facing mine. I mumbled,

"Now what are you doing?" I strained to see for myself through the filtered light from the curtained windows what she was now doing.

"Nothing," she said, "I'm trying to sleep."

"But there is somebody at the foot of your bed."

"Well it's not me," she responded and at that moment the apparition literally faded backward through the door and yep, we went to sleep. My sisters have had their own spirit world experiences. We know when to perk up and fight (yes, sometimes, you fight!) and we know when to just let it go. It is strange I will admit, but we often can very clearly decipher or discern when a spirit is evil and when it is not. For that I am most grateful.

Oh! The next morning when my sister called to wake us up around 6 a.m. she told us Daddy had arrested again around midnight. Yet again they had "brought him back."

Talking about Daddy dying in 1988 causes me to recall his first open heart surgery ten years earlier. It was scheduled to be performed at Shands Memorial

Hospital in Gainesville, Florida. He had asked me to drive down and be present. I immediately made plans to go, but I had a dilemma. Money was short, and I needed a large dust free hotel room or suite that was clean and cheap. It had to be big enough to accommodate all my siblings as we came and went and took naps and assisted in Daddy's care as needed. Daddy had told me the name of a street that had a lot of hotel choices near the hospital, and that the area was, in his opinion, safer so I drove there first, before I ever went to the hospital.

Yep, I was in search of the perfect hotel room. Clean and dust free also was imperative because I am asthmatic and highly allergic. I found the recommended street and immediately spotted several major hotels. I pulled into a major gas station to refill my gas tank before beginning my search. Next to me was a man who also appeared to be searching for something. While the gas flowed, his and mine, he had a big book open on the hood of his car and was flipping through the pages. I interrupted him and asked if he was familiar with the area.

He said, "Yes, can I help you?"

I said, "Yessir, I am looking for a clean, affordable hotel, the cleanest one I can possibly find."

"Why?" he asked.

I told my story.

He said, "Well, miss, I am not supposed to make recommendations like this, but in your case, I am going to make an exception. I work for the state of Florida and I inspect hotels. That's what this book before me is all about. There's one just a few blocks from here, over by the interstate, that is so clean you could eat off the floor, plus rates are very reasonable. Go there and explain your need to the manager, but don't mention me."

I did what he said and rented a most extraordinary suite that served my family well for nearly two weeks. I think the guy was real. I know his book was thick and very real. He was indeed pumping gas into a vehicle, but I often have wondered if he was an angel.

CHAPTER FOURTEEN

Many aspects of my life are reasonably normal. Healthwise, I have struggled. Throughout life my allergies have been such that I eventually learned to just laugh and tell folks that God Himself must have sneezed and accidentally sent me to the wrong planet. Laughter is good, but it does not come easily for me. That was a nice thing I quickly learned to appreciate about television. When we got our first set, I was quite young, and it introduced me to "My Little Margie" and "Our Miss Brooks." A few years later "I Love Lucy" came along. They made me laugh! I do not think I had laughed much prior to seeing those programs. It felt good. In fact, hard laughter would trigger coughing that would promote vomiting which allowed me to expel much of the phlegm that was forever building up in my lungs. I have a barrel chest today and my fingertips are clubbed. That happens to severe asthmatics sometimes. I spent a lot of time in the hospital as a kid.

On the day I picked up this new laptop computer on which I am typing these very words, my sister told the Best Buy store manager that I was giving this little machine to myself as a birthday present. That was true. Then she continued and told him about how my mother always kept pencil and paper handy when I was little. She would see that I had it with me inside so many of the cold damp oxygen tents of my youth. Drawing, as a preschooler, then later writing, kept me calm. It helped me not to panic as I fought for air.

I recall quite clearly that I was five years old when I took charge of my own body and my health. The nurse came in around noon to stick my finger again and get blood for yet another lab test. I told her no. She had stuck me several days in a row and I was tired of it.

She begged.

I said no.

My mom begged.

I said no.

The nurse said she would have to call the doctor if I did not cooperate.

I said, "Go do that and tell him that if I can have a break from your needle today that you can stick me tomorrow and I won't ever cry again."

She left.

She came back.

She said, "The doctor said that sounded like a good deal." It was. All around.

CHAPTER FIFTEEN

I have never cried since that day because of a needle or a scalpel or any kind of medical procedure and I have had plenty of occasions to do so, but I promised. I keep my promises. And that is why I finally published "Malignant Emotion," in 2009.

In May of that year, five years after Cindy's death, I had power surge after power surge one week. Lost five pieces of technical equipment. A television. A fax machine. A printer. Two computers. What still worked was riddled with white noise. I was truly puzzled and during the week, as all of this was happening, I remembered that it was the five-year anniversary of Cindy's death. I also remembered my promise to publish that "novel." You cannot imagine how much I did not want to do it. That writing was private for me. My gift to just her. A treasure exchanged between two friends who had shared much over the years. But I had promised. It was and forever will be my only deathbed promise. Not going there again!

So, I opened the file, started formatting it and published it through Create Space. I was working with a lady at the time, Janet, who was president of a breast cancer support organization and I told her about Cindy and how she had been diagnosed in her late 20s with breast cancer. I talked about her journey at length. Janet is a survivor as well. I told her Cindy had both breasts removed in the very beginning and went into remission only to have the cancer recur about ten years later. I remember it well because she had just started on the drug, tamoxifen, and I was visiting her on the Darton College Campus in Albany, GA. We were walking along on a paved walk when she decided to cut across the grass. I stayed on the pavement. She said, "Cut across."

I said, "No, I don't want to kill the grass."

She said, "Well that grass is gonna live longer than me. I'm taking every shortcut I can."

I'm not sure how long the grass lived, but she went into remission yet again. Then in her early fifties it returned with a vengeance.

I am not saying that Cindy or any spirits she may have inspired were responsible for what was happening to all my electronics that year, but I decided to not take any chances and get the darn book done. Janet showed a real interest in it and invited me to be a guest speaker at a few events. Cindy was one of three close friends who had died with breast cancer at that point. Jackie and Maxine were the other two. You are going to hear a lot about Maxine a little later. So, I got the book done and printed a thousand copies. Janet and I loaded a few hundred into the car and headed south to my first promotional speaking engagement. We met our hostess for dinner on Friday night and she gave us an overview of what was ahead for the next day. That night, on our way back to our hotel, we were in a head on collision.

And this is where things get a bit sticky… or stickier. Hard for me to understand. Very. Even harder to share for many reasons.

I was driving a Honda Pilot. Those who test such things said it was the safest car on the road that year. I was approaching a traffic light that was green. Another car was, as well. As we got closer to the light, I observed that the driver of the oncoming vehicle accelerated his speed and was going to attempt to turn in front of me. I slammed on my breaks, but it was too late. In seconds, his small car was sitting on top of my front bumper. I could see under the streetlights that a young blond kid was driving. Then suddenly he started laughing. Unbelievable laughter that I could hear through our windows and I certainly could see it.

My friend Janet, said, "Do you see that?"

I said yes.

"That guy. The kid driving. Do you see his face?" she asked.

Again, I said yes.

"It changed," she said.

"I know, tell me what you see," I responded.

She described what I also was seeing and hearing.

Then quickly the big, very dark grotesque visual that had become his face morphed back to the kid's normal blond appearance, but the hysterically heinous laughter continued.

By that time, a police officer was at my window. He had been sitting at the intersection, stopped because his side of the light was red. He opened my car door and asked if I was okay. I said yes. "Then let's get you and your friend out of this car before your air bags belatedly deploy. Sometimes they do that, and you can get hurt."

I turned to step from the car and the pain hit. Like nothing I had ever experienced. It spread from my waistline in my back up to my neck and down to my sacrum and then around into my diaphragm. Oh, God, how it hurt. The officer called for an ambulance.

The kid was still laughing. Blond again. The officer kept glancing over at him. He was out of his car by then and laughing so very loudly. The cop looked at me and said, "I am sorry ma'am. Some people respond strangely to events like this. Laughter like that may be his way of coping." I did not know what to say, so I said nothing. The kid was walking around laughing crazily. But at least he was still blonde.

When the ambulance arrived, the medics wanted me to lie down on the stretcher. That was impossible. The pain was too bad. The officer said I had to lie down, that I could not sit up on the stretcher. I asked him to please see if my car was drivable. He checked and backed it out from under the kid's car and said he thought it was. I said, "Ok, then I think I can sit down in the passenger seat and let my friend drive me around to the hospital."

That's what we did. The place was full of patients with flu. The nurse in me, whether I was using good sense or not, suddenly envisioned me as a patient with flu, coughing and sneezing amidst the horrific spasms in my neck and back and diaphragm that I already knew had come to stay for a while, although I truly had no idea what lay ahead. No idea at all.

I turned to Janet and said, "Let's leave. I cannot afford to catch flu." I could not bear the thought of a ten-day cough while in such pain.

"But what will we do for your pain?

"Let's go buy me some beer," I said. I'm not a

heavy drinker so I knew a few swallows would relax me. It literally only takes only half a beer or about four swallows of wine to sedate me, even put me to sleep.

Janet protested. She had never purchased liquor. Not in her whole life, she said. Luckily, we found a drive through liquor store and I made the purchase through the window. I called a friend and asked her to bring me a muscle relaxer to take the next day for my ride home. I figured I could take it after I spoke at the event, then I would see my doctor on Monday. She drove over to our hotel with the pill and found me sitting on the side of the bed guzzling my second beer and in excruciating pain.

She and Janet lifted my legs and helped me stretch out on the bed, where I final dozed. I sipped beer the following morning prior to my talk. I also smiled and gracefully greeted all who were in attendance. That is what a proper southern lady does. She keeps her obligations. Yeah, I'm laughing too, at that one. Proper I am not! I reckon you have already guessed that.

I remember selling a copy of "Malignant Emotion" to the wife of a Baptist preacher that day. I winced as I took her money and whispered softly, "Please don't burn it until you read the whole thing." She looked puzzled. Later she emailed me and said she had not understood why I had said that at the event. When she contacted me, after finishing the book, she said she had started loaning it out. She said she wished every member of her church could read it. That was a pleasant shock!

Once the autographing was over, I swallowed the muscle relaxer my friend had brought and we left for home.

Janet got a speeding ticket.

I went to see my doctor on Monday. She gave me a legal prescription for the same muscle relaxer. I still did not realize hell had come down. Oh, but… I just sucked it up. Resolved that the pain would pass in time. I had work to do. Appearances to make. Appointments to keep. Books to sell. The pain was horrific.

A few weeks later, I drove to Nashville for an inspirational country music convention. When I checked into my hotel, the clerk asked if I was in town for surgery at Vanderbilt. I reckon the pain was rather apparent after that six-hour drive. I said no that I was working. He offered to bring in my luggage. I appreciated it.

Two nights later, I was sitting in the audience at the convention where we were enjoying a series of 15 minute to 30 minute showcases. I was familiar with most of the artists, but I had never heard of Steve Richard before that night. He was booked for around 9 or 9:30. My head was literally throbbing beyond description. I was sitting about five rows back from the stage where I could take good pictures and hear everything that was said. As harsh as the lights were, they permitted me to take good notes. I was still writing my column at the time.

Suddenly the curtains lifted, and oh my! Oh, oh, oh my! A very different kind of music permeated the place. Loudly. The singer was a quite polished performer and he belted out lyrics that simply were not a fit for the setting. Not at all. Folks all over the auditorium started popping up and heading to the front of the building, looking for the president of the organization hosting these showcases. I am told there are people who furiously left that night, canceled their memberships, and never returned. Me? I just sat still, listening and watching and praying that my head would not burst. Finally, the very loud band stopped playing, the artist bowed and left the stage.

THAT's when it happened. I truly could not believe it. Totally pissed me off. The little voice of mine (not at all audible) that often prompts actions I would not ordinarily choose, very clearly said, "Go to him. Thank him for the performance. Tell him God has given him a tremendous gift and that you are from Georgia and if he is ever in the Atlanta area at a more appropriate venue then you would like to hear him again."

"Oh, hell no." That was a no brainer. I think I may have even muttered those words aloud, but only to myself.

The message came again. Exactly as I just stated.

Once more, I said no.

Again, it came.

So, I am arguing silently with this irritating voice in my spirit and I say silently, "Look he is a recording artist. He mentioned his bus while on stage. Buses are parked in a special secure area that I cannot access."

"His is not. It's right behind your car," whispered the silent voice.

"No, it is not. I'm parked in the handicap parking area."

"Go look. His bus is right behind your car."

"Can't be. Besides its raining."

"Go."

"No."

"And take a copy of your book 'You are Somebody and I am, too.'"

"Seriously?"

"Give him the book and give him the message, word for word."

Well at that point I was downright angry, but also, I had grown super curious. My Maker knows me well. He knows what will motivate me to act. At that point I had a double helping of curiosity and anger contained inside a head that felt like it would explode at any moment. The pain was atrocious.

I went.

Sure enough. The bus was right there, parked directly behind my car. The singer was already in it. What looked like the driver was still outside. I quickly got the book out of my car, went to him, and asked to speak to Steve. He went inside the big fancy bus and got him. I gave him the message. Oh, my goodness! Apparently, all he heard was "more appropriate venue!"

"What do you mean 'more appropriate venue?' This place is great. I reserved this showcase spot for that very reason. It's the perfect place…"

Or something to that effect. I don't remember his exact words, but I do remember mine and I had said them, so I wished him well, said goodbye, walked back through the rain and went inside while he went back into his bus.

Whew, that had been interesting...

I returned to my seat and to softer, more soothing sounds although I could still sense that the "Christian" crowd remained somewhat unnerved by what many of them had deemed highly inappropriate lyrics and music for the setting.

About thirty minutes later, I looked up to see Steve Richard step around the curtain with his gorgeous wife's hand in his. He eased down the steps and walked along the outside of the wall toward the front of the building. After a few minutes, he and the same guy who would later, in 2014, introduce me to JesseLee Jones stepped back on the stage and asked for the crowd's attention. Steve apologized. He had no idea what was going on there. He was not a member of the organization. He had just needed to book that stage and do a showcase.

At the last minute, his dad had flown in and Steve had changed up the songs without getting the organization's approval. He picked songs he thought his dad might better enjoy. He was humble. Kind. Deeply apologetic. And all the other artists backstage embraced him with open arms. He became a member of the organization. Later, I heard him say publicly how that was the only one he ever joined that did not kick him out.

Later, Steve recorded two songs that blessed me beyond measure. His rendition of "Eighty Acre Church" thrilled both my husband and me! And the message of "Love's Gotta Go Somewhere" touches my life daily. I cherish the impact Steve Richard has had on my life and the lives of so many others.

Don't ask me how this matters in the grand scheme of things or in any kind of eternal spectrum. I do not have a clue. I just tell my stories and let the words fall where they will. I don't have to understand or put it all together.

THOSE MOMENTS THAT MATTER

Throwing all caution to the wind
I let my words fall where they may
I let my heart write what it would say
To people everywhere
Who long to know they are not alone
Even when loved ones are suddenly gone
Hopes crushed and dreams shattered
Though all that ever mattered
Lies broken at their feet
I hope my words will fall there, too
Like rose petals of promise
Whose fragrance wafts upward
Into the recesses of the soul
Which would refuse to face another day
If it were not for these words
My heart so longs to say

God's grace is sufficient
His love everlasting
His way not always our way
Is what I would say
To that one who fears to face tomorrow
Were God's judgments not tempered
With unending mercy
None could withstand
The touch of His hand
But His hand reaches down
Not to hurt or destroy
Because of the anger I know He must feel
Since our mistakes and failures are so very real

THOSE MOMENTS THAT MATTER

Instead
His hand reaches out to you and to me
To guide us gently
When there's not enough light to see
The path which lies before us
Or glimpse the goal that's just ahead
When there is not enough faith to envision
A victory on some distant shore
When there is only anger and anguish and pain
When it seems there is no way to win
And nothing to gain
By continuing to trudge along in this world
Then
That hand
His hand
Reaches out to touch His own
And with a gentle nudge that's His alone
He turns His children toward the Morning Light
With a firm assurance once again
That the darkness they have known for so long
Will soon know its appointed end

Indeed
I must throw all caution to the wind
And let my pen fall where it may
For in the end
I, too, find hope
In what my heart does long to say

CHAPTER SIXTEEN

About those stories that I tell… and the fact that I kinda don't care what people might say or think about them. Back in my late thirties I got accused of having an affair with someone who was very dear to me, someone I truly loved. I dearly loved his wife as well, and nothing sexually inappropriate ever took place between him and me. But we were much closer in spirit than most folks find comfortable. Especially strait-laced judgmental Christian types.

So one day, in the work setting in which this relationship had been birthed, I showed up one morning to find that all the ladies who worked there had put chairs in a circle and they had Bibles in hand prayerfully waiting for me. They asked me to sit down and then they confronted me "biblically" about what they perceived to be my transgression. I listened and did not open my mouth to defend myself. That is probably as close as I will ever come to knowing how Jesus must have felt when he faced his false accusers, because He and all of heaven knows I've been guilty of enough stuff about which I have never been confronted. Therefore I could never really understand the plight of Jesus. Nevertheless, that was an interesting and most unforgettable day, a day filled with moments that mattered much and certainly shaped my life going forward!

When I walked out of the makeshift courtroom that day, I resolved to never give a damn again about what anybody thought of me. I figured they are going to think whatever they want to think based on their perception of their very limited observations - whoever "they" may be on any given day, and they also will try to entertain themselves and others with their talk, gossip, that is, based on their judgments. The best way I know to look at it is maybe some other poor soul is getting a break while whomever "they" may be focus their narrowminded and occasionally venomous misjudgments on me. I sure hope I'm not sounding too high and mighty as I type these words because trust me, I've done my share of wrongful judgment, as well. Plus, like I just said, I have done much that is more than worthy of criticism, things nobody ever knew anything about. The truth is "what goes around comes around." I reckon it was my turn that day for it to come back around to me. I have tried to be not so judgmental since then. I found out how much it hurts to be wrongly accused. I try… but even with the small measure of extrasensory insights that are mine, I still fall short of fully understanding and extending grace to other folks, and I know I judge them quite harshly on occasion. Some day that whole concept of "grace" will sink in a little better. At least, I hope it will. I am thankful for it. I want others to experience it, even Hillary Clinton.

CHAPTER SEVENTEEN

I'm not sure why I just chose to mention HRC in my personal memoir. There are many people who are part of our personal stories to some degree that we might wish were not, not even out in the fringe areas. I have never met Hillary Clinton. I do not care to. The list of reasons why I have no respect for her is quite long, but the absolute final straw for me was when she said that I and many women like me, voted for Donald Trump because our husbands told us we had to do it. That was a bit much. Might be forgivable. Might not. I'm working on it. Of course, she was already on thin ice with many moms like me because of "Benghazi 9/11/12."

Actually, the last statesman for whom I had a reasonable degree of respect was Senator Sam Nunn, Democrat from Georgia. Many of us Georgians wanted him to run for president. He refused to put his family through such an ordeal back then. Can you imagine what he would say today, now that politicians on all sides, for the most part, have collectively lost their minds? (It's 2020 as I type these words.)

I voted for Donald Trump in 2016 because I felt like he would shake up Washington, DC. He did, from day one. He has continued to do so every day since. I perceived that he had the potential to enter the presidency like an indiscriminate and somewhat clumsy bull in a china shop ready to take wild inventory. He has not disappointed in that respect. I detest the impotent refusal to work together for the common good that has taken root in Congress and among elected officials all over my country.

Does anybody have a backbone anymore? Is there any respect for law and order left? Trump has made mistakes. The thing that most irritates me about him is the disrespect for others that so easily rolls off his tongue or fingers into his Twitter feed. He is, after all, President of the United States, and many of the people he criticizes, and makes fun of, are my fellow citizens. Like Trump, I may not agree with them, but I respect their story, their history. I want to better understand where they come from. I cringe when he speaks, but I comfort myself with reminders that at least he is not part of the Washington, DC status quo that has stepped on my last nerve and yours, too, perhaps. While I don't care for his tweets and some of his spoken comments, I am thankful for a lot that he actually has done. On that note, I am watch Gov. Scott Walker from afar. I think I like him.

Maybe these political comments I have allowed on this page is a good a way as any to make myself back up a bit to 2007. If I'm going to talk about angels in the midst of demons dancing on the broad ways of our lives, then 2007 must have its say.

God help me.

She was my neighbor and I had met her a few days before Christmas, 2006. We were standing in front of a beautifully decorated Christmas tree that we both admired together silently. Aloud, I asked her where she was from. They, she and her husband, had just moved to town and were building a new home, out in the country, right down from me. She said she was lonely, and I asked about her interests. I offered to host a luncheon after Christmas and introduce her to a few local ladies with similar hobbies and interests. I later became ill, with excruciating back pain, and had to cancel. I saw her again three more times before she died. Each time, I made excuses for how busy I was planning a big fundraiser and working part time. At our last encounter, I asked her to please bear with me. I told her that my big event would soon be over and after April 17th I would have all the time in the world for her, and we would get to know one another. She took her own life on April 4th.

Ever since then when I hear people talk about the first person they want to see in heaven, I always think of her. She is at the top of my list. Even now as I type these words, the tears are welling up and the lump in my throat is almost unbearable. I failed her. Miserably. She changed my life. Eternally. Everything changed with her death. It was the most profound paradigm shift of my life. On the morning of her death, I drove by her home at 9:15. My little voice said to stop. I refused. I had things to do.

The truth is it was the only day since Christmas that I'd had all to myself and I wanted to drive some country back roads and look for a measure of peace and tranquility, and just relax. That afternoon when I returned home, I was in my back yard, around 2 p.m., not sure of the exact time, but I heard the sirens. I would not know until two days later that her husband had come home and found her dead from a self-inflicted gunshot wound.

I am incapable of describing the anguish that consumed me following her death. The guilt was almost unbearable. The abject sense of failure was nauseatingly painful. Still is, at times. I tried to make up for it by reaching out to her grieving husband. He became my project. I felt like I had to keep him alive since I had failed to keep her alive.

Guys, I am sorry, but I just have to let the words fall where they will if I'm going to talk about angels and demons and the spirit world. I really did not give a lot of thought to demonic warfare prior to 2007. In February of that year, a locally appointed female political official contacted me and asked me to speak on her behalf as a group of male county commissioners plotted to fire her "because she was a woman."

The hearing was at the local courthouse. I had already called all the commissioners in protest and I attended the meeting. I spoke there as well. I pleaded. I knew she had a humdinger of a lawsuit. I knew it would cost the county a lot of money. I knew it would sour her on a career in which she had always shined. They fired her anyway with a courtroom full of protesters. She sued. It cost the county a lot of money. And she also changed professions. But that day, in that courthouse as angry citizens started climbing over the benches to verbally attack the commissioners, I stepped to the front of the room where the sheriff was attempting to guard the wayward officials and asked everybody to join hands and have prayer. I had no idea what I was doing. Really. No idea at all.

I did not know about territorial spirits and I certainly did not know I was opening myself up to an all-out attack, but I did so that day. There is much that I still do not understand. I do know that, in the midst of caring for my family, standing with the lady who was fired, planning the big fundraiser, etc. I'd had a dream. It was prophetic. I knew it was. It was awful. It foretold death. Later, on April 4th, as I drove by my neighbor's house, the fog and feeling was exactly like what had been in my dream. I should have stopped. I did not. As I drove by my neighbor's home, a whoosh of heavy greyness entered my car. Like the fog itself had found a way into the vehicle. Later I would learn that her time of death was placed at approximately 9:15 a.m.

How is my neighbor's suicide tied to the courtroom scene and so much else that happened from Christmas 2006 to July 5, 2010? I don't know. I just know that my life became a living hell on earth during that period with demons dancing in and out of my life at will. I must speak of my neighbor though I did not know her long because as the songs goes, *"If anyone should ever write my life story, for whatever reason there might be…"* she will be there between every line. While I only knew her those few short months, there is no aspect of my life she has not influenced since her death.

CHAPTER EIGHTEEN

From Christmas of 2006 when I first met my neighbor until July 2, 2010 my life was tormented. Yes, it started before I called for the prayer meeting in the old courthouse where much corruption had once reigned. In looking back, I think everything was already in play before I met my new neighbor, before the county official asked for my help, and well before I foolishly assumed authority where I had none. That said, and please believe me when I tell you this, because this is one of those things of which I am certain. God already had a plan to use it all for the good of many.

Let me assure you that I do not always like the ways I see God's will revealed. I certainly do not understand it and no way would I choose to make things happen like they so often do. But I do choose. You do, too. We all do and collectively we set things in motion that must evolve based on the choices we make. How God manages to work it all out for the good of those who are called according to His purposes, I do not have a clue. That is above my pay grade. But he does it. I promise He does.

Indirectly because of my neighbor's husband, I ended up doing radio and television. I hated doing TV, truly despised it, but loved radio. Loved playing inspirational country music and talking about the songs and artists who sang them. That led to my creating and producing a little program called "Reach to Touch" where for about five years now I've been interviewing folks and talking with them about their creative works and how their books and films and songs are used to touch lives all around the world.

Interestingly, my voice is heard literally all around the world now. Around 1987, I wrote a poem titled "I want To Go Home," that I knew was autobiographical even as the ink leaked from my pen. It was strange and it was so long that I actually used it as my column at the time of the writing. I will share it with you at some point, but first I need to tell you about Maxine.

If you are trying at this point to connect a few dots and make sense out of my life story so far, have at it. Please know that I am not. I do not care to do that. I don't like outlines, or schedules, or to do lists, or going and coming the same way from any destination. Thanks to my neighbor and to Cindy, in part perhaps, I have come to more or less enjoy a much looser, less manipulative approach to life. But the truth is ... none of those attempts at organization works for me. Life can still blow up in my face, break my heart, bring on a health crisis, and take my loved ones from me. So I just live freely and as spontaneously as possible, and let that inner voice lead me as best I can along an often strange and ever-winding path.

I often think WHAT IF… what if the first time I ever became aware of the voice, what if I had listened and followed directions every single time? I wonder about much. It is enough to know that I listen and follow more closely now than ever before. Oh, and there is the fact that I was a nurse for 18 years and my first assignment out of nursing school was to a psychiatric ward as nightshift supervisor so I learned early on what normal people thought about folks who could hear voices. Even though mine was not audible it was still real and way more than a random thought. So very much more!

CHAPTER NINETEEN

Probably the most important thing at this point in time and in my life as it presently is unfolding on earth, is the fact that I do attempt to be a Christ follower, (though some days I'd sure hate to know how I am being graded). It was not always that way. In fact, I grew up pretending to be a Christian while secretly, I was jealous of Jesus Christ, downright offended that He somehow got to be called "God's only begotten son." I knew for a fact that I was God's kid, too. Talk about sibling rivalry, I was consumed by it at times.

As I said earlier, I grew up with my share of hell fire and brimstone threats. I knew to pray daily, said all the right words in my prayers, too, "right words" according to the folks who were trying to inject their belief systems and theology into my heart and life. I was required to memorize scripture from the bible. However, when I was old enough, I began to study other religions, secretly, that is. My family would never have cottoned to the idea of such open-mindedness.

For me there was just too much that did not fit. I never outgrew my connection, however, to the God from Whom I felt I had come. I still feel that way. Sometimes I think I can still remember being "with God" before I came here. SO, I suppose that brings me to two things that probably have most influenced my life so far, as it has unfolded and probably will continue to unfold. Those things would be (1) my attitude about death and (2) my belief about purpose.

First, let's talk about purpose. An awareness of purpose is important if we are to maintain a present and active state of mind. In Rick Warren's book "The Purpose Driven Life" (which I highly recommend), he says that knowing our purpose motivates our life because purpose produces passion. I could not agree more. In the front of my Bible I once wrote:

The greatest blasphemy is to say "God, I love you, it just doesn't excite me." I would take that a step further now and say, "The greatest disservice you can do to yourself is to say "Life, I love you, you just don't excite me." Now, whose fault would that be?

As a kid and well into my adult years, my greatest fear was of boredom. The thought that I might one day wake up bored terrified me. My slate is so full now, and my never-ending list of things to do is so long, that I do not live with that fear any longer!

While there is much I speculate about, (truly, there are not many places I won't let my forever wondering and pondering mind go…) I am not afraid. It is hard to be aware of that God connection and be afraid at the same time. But what I speculate about and what I truly BELIEVE with every fiber of my being... well, they have not always jived. In fact, over time I have released many of the things I have speculated about or pondered on. If they took me nowhere promising, I let them go. Doesn't mean I didn't enjoy the ride. I just got off sooner or later. BUT my belief which has finally come to me along with my recognition of my purpose on earth is that Jesus loves me. I once wrote ever so simplistically:

> Jesus loves me, this I know
> Why He loves me, I don't know.
> But tell me,
> What more do I need to know?

When I came to that realization, my life changed. Peace and Hope moved into my heart, set up camp, and never took it down. There is a lot more I want to know, oh yeah, but I don't feel the NEED to know it, like I once did.

The Jesus and me thing may be kind of like you wanting your mom or dad to love and accept you – or a sibling or somebody with whom there's just always been this measure of tension you would like to remove. Coming to a point where I really believed Jesus loved me and feeling free to love Him in turn was a BIG DEAL for me!

I suppose there are a million things I could tell you

about where I come from and who I am, but nothing ever impacted my spiritual earth history like the story I am about to tell you.

It was in the 1970's, and I was still clinging to church attendance as a means to an end, and some days even an end in itself. I am not sure I even understand exactly what I mean by that, but my heart tells me that's about as true a statement as I can make regarding attending church. I was just trying to get it right. I was baptized twice, at age 16 because everybody else did it, and because some preacher preached a sermon about "God is love" that really got to me!

At 23, I got baptized again, that time I was just trying to wash away the guilt of having been three months pregnant when I married – well, that guilt and maybe a little more. But it didn't work. I mean, my dad was a Baptist preacher, after all. Did I really think water could wash away that kind of Bible Belt guilt from 1968? There simply was no peace. All the Jesus stuff just didn't set well with me. Yeah, I was still jealous. In all honesty, it was just hard for me to believe it – the Jesus story, or stories, that is, and it always had been.

But I stayed in church. I kept studying my bible and other religions, too. I am still intrigued by other faiths, and respectful of them, as well. The truth is, even now, I did not and do not find all the answers that I seek. I just found peace. The day I found it – well, that was the day I accepted Jesus. I'm guessing that "accepting Jesus" may not mean the same to me that it means to some of you, but it is the way it was, so I will tell you about it.

When my sons were around six and eight years old, they did not want to go to Sunday School any longer, because Daddy didn't go. "Why should we go if he does not?" is what they asked me. Repeatedly.

It was a legitimate question. I pondered on that question a long time. Prayed about it the best I knew how to pray. One day, after pacing up and down my hallway, then kneeling at an ottoman in my living room which had become my personal altar, the phone rang. It was Pastor Joseph Dimazo, a Seventh Day Adventist pastor who fate had brought into my life the year before. Following our meeting this remarkable man phoned me several times. No more than six or seven all total, I'd say, though I do not recall exactly. But each time he called I would be at that ottoman or pacing the hall of my home in prayer. Each and every single time! That's weird because I did not really pray all that much back then. And each time he would say he was in his study and that God had placed me on his heart, and that he was praying for me. He wanted to know if I had specific prayer requests or if there was anything I needed to talk about.

That day, I explained my dilemma. I told him what a good dad my husband was. How I wanted his sons to admire and respect him. How I did not want to appear to them as being smarter or better or wiser or whatever… than their dad, especially with them being boys, and one day growing to be a man like their dad whom I adored. Of course, I do not remember all I said – not my exact words – to Pastor Dimazo that day. I just know I poured out my heart. He had invited me to do so. I felt perfect freedom with him to do just that, which is strange, because, like I said, I had only met with him in person once. That was at the Atlanta Farmer's Market. Earlier, before I had ever met him, I had spent a week with my dad at a Seventh Day Adventist hospital when he had been treated following his first heart attack. I had been so impressed with the place and staff that I wanted to know more about the religion. When I returned to Atlanta, I looked up the Adventist churches in the phone book and started calling the numbers to find a church representative who could help me in an effort to better educate myself. If I have a super strong suit in my efforts to live life well, I am guessing it is tied to my insatiable curiosity.

Pastor Dimazo was the only pastor with whom I

made contact that day. He and his wife offered to meet me at Thomas's Restaurant at the Farmer's Market and answer any questions I might have. I accepted the invitation and that was it, the only time I ever saw him in person.

But then the phone calls started.

SO – back to my story. Pastor Dimazo said to me. "Mary Jane, I have never told anyone to stop going to church, but clearly that is what God is leading you to do and you must do it. Follow His leadership always. No matter what others may say. No matter what." I will never forget the way he said God's name. "God" had a different sound to it when Pastor Dimazo said it. The name of God meaning "I Am" gave me a new perspective when Pastor Dimazo so reverently spoke that name above all names. It was like the "I AM" was ever present, everywhere, and knew everything. He sure told Pastor Dimazo exactly when to call me.

Anyway, that may have been the first time I started to glimpse the importance of truly practicing living in the moment, experiencing the present completely, going with the flow of who I was, where I was, and how I was evolving in each and every present moment of my life.

CHAPTER TWENTY

I stopped going to church and began to read the bible to my sons at home. I took personal responsibility for my sons' religious education. Yep. A first! I'd left all that up the Church until that time. So, the three of us started to study Bible stories together and talk philosophy. (To this day, my sons can hold their own in such conversation!) After a few months, a call came one day from a woman named Maxine Carter. I knew of her. I had seen her around at the church I had attended but did not really know her at all.

She had called to tell me she was starting a Thursday morning Bible Study and that she knew my story. By then, everybody at that church knew my story! I'm pretty sure my name had been moved to the top of several prayer lists when I made my choice to drop church. I did not just stop going. I had announced my decision my last time in Sunday School first. Sure did. So anyway, Maxine suggested that there would be no conflict with my sons and their respect for their dad and all, if I wanted to come to her Bible Study. They would, after all, be in school and their dad at work and whatever I decided was fine. No pressure. None. Just an invite.

I thought about it for a few days before I accepted.

Then I went every Thursday morning for nine months to study the Book of John. For those of you who do not know it already, that New Testament book is often called The Book of Belief.

I learned over time that there was good reason for it being called that. Later we would study the book of Philippians, and also Genesis, neither of which did all that much for me. In retrospect, it was that Book of John and Maxine that got to me, started to put me into an eternally present spiritual state of mind.

John's writings about Jesus had me thinking that Jesus really was something special. And Maxine, well, she just accepted me. No judgments. No questioning. No third-degree type religious stuff. Just acceptance. Over time and several tests that I put her through I realized I was experiencing unconditional love for the first time in my life.

Many of us are blessed to be loved to some degree by somebody at one time or another, but most folks who claim to love us, and who really do love as much as they are capable of loving us, usually expect something in return. That is okay. It's just the way it is. Our parents, our significant others, our children, siblings, friends – they all expect things from us. That's life. We expect certain behavior, certain actions, certain responses, etc. from others as well.

But for the first time ever in my life I had encountered someone who was just letting me be me – scars and all. No question I ever asked shocked her. Anything I said was okay. Like the night I wore inappropriate red short shorts to her bible study, just to see if she would still love me…, it was like she never even saw them. All she saw was the heart and soul of me. And she clearly loved me. NO MATTER WHAT. I was blessed! Changed.

Then, a couple of years after I had first attended her home bible study, she got sick again. I say again because though she never talked much about, I knew she'd had breast cancer several years before. Of course, nobody thought the cancer was back. About the time she started to feel bad, she went to Israel, a trip she had planned for a long time. But while she was gone, she grew sicker. When she returned, she was hospitalized, and it was determined that she had hepatitis. She grew sicker and sicker. One night a group of us from the Bible Study went to her home to clean house for her. When she meted out assignments, she did not ask me to do anything.

After the others left the room, she asked me to close the door and sit down. Then she proceeded to tell me that God had shown her many things about me. She talked long. I listened with what smidgeon of faith and awareness I had at the time, but to this day there is only one thing I remember vividly.

During that conversation when she was so weak and frail, and it was so hard for her to communicate at all, she told me God was going to call me to a "special work." I do not recall asking her anything about the special work. I just remember laughing and somewhat mockingly saying "and tell me then what God is going to do with my husband when He calls me to this special work?"

She said, "Don't worry. God will take care of Daniel in every way." (At Daniel's death, decades later, his faith was much deeper than mine.)

I heard her out and felt pretty stupid sitting there while everybody else worked. Felt stupid, that is, until sometime later when I realized that I had been blessed that night to personally experience the wisdom and beauty of the Martha and Mary story as recorded in chapter 10 of John's Gospel. (You can make a note: John 10 and look it up later if you'd like. We won't go there now.)

A few days went by and Maxine got sicker. The Bible Study group planned to meet together to pray for her. I got in the shower late that afternoon, before our prayer meeting time. There is something really cleansing and therapeutic about crying in a shower ... try it sometime! As I stood there crying, praying, so desperately wanting her well again, the little voice spoke to me. Yep, that little voice that hides in some level of my consciousness and had been speaking to me all my life – often giving me direction. Not that I always followed those directions. Offering comfort. Not that I always accepted the comfort that was offered. Speaking peace to my sometimes-troubled heart and soul. Not that I even wanted peace back then. Sometimes, turmoil just fit me better. I think I thought I could learn more from the turmoil. And always I hungered to learn more. Since the voice had been with me forever, I reckon it was one of the reasons I felt like I didn't really need Jesus. God loved me anyway and I knew it.

Well, that day in the shower, several bible verses began to flow into my mind. Almost like they were being spoken aloud to some place deep inside my troubled heart that knew it had to listen. I quickly got out of the shower. Wrapped myself in a towel and headed for my bible to look up the words. Had to verify the truth of what was being said to me. Didn't like what I was hearing. Crying hard, I found them. I did indeed find those words! Exactly as they had come to me in the shower. Those words found in Mark 4:29 had never really meant anything to me – until that day. They were:

"But when the crop permits, he immediately puts in the sickle, because the harvest has come."

In that instant as I read and heard those words aloud in my own voice, not the one from the shower, I knew that Maxine would die shortly. She died within a week. It turned out to be cancer again. Not hepatitis.

On the day of her funeral, I drove away from the church with my heart breaking. Shattering. I knew what I had found in her, and I knew what I had lost with her passing, and I knew something else. I knew the source of the unconditional love she had so consistently exhibited towards me. As I drove away from the church that day, alone in my car, tears falling. I heard myself talking out loud to Jesus, no less. Not God. Jesus!

I heard myself saying, "Okay, I believe it. I believe You are everything You ever claimed to be and more. I believe You love me. And now that I have seen that kind of love in action, I really don't think I can live without it. Will You be my friend?" I had pulled off by the side of the road only a mile or so from my home to have this conversation.

I had covered the savior part earlier, at eight years old, when I had heard a terrifying sermon about hell. I'm still striving about His lordship role. And I'm certainly still not a model Christian so I hope you know better than to just follow me. Follow Him, please.

But that day, as imperfect as I was, and still am, Jesus became my friend. He may have been "with me" all my life. His spirit – that is. His presence. I don't know. I just know that the Presence I began to feel that day, as I talked with Him alone in my car, is still with me today. I know there has never been a time, since that day in October 1978, that I have doubted His existence and his unconditional love for me.

CHAPTER TWENTY-ONE

Now, for my attitude about death...

Like I said earlier: There are two things that probably have most influenced my life here and the way it has unfolded and probably will continue to unfold. Those things would be (1) my attitude about death and (2) my belief about purpose.

Maxine's death, and the death of my neighbor who committed suicide, showed me personally that even death has its purposes. In death we can sometimes impact the world even more than we did in what we perceive to be life. And the influence goes on and on. Death is not an end. It is just a transitional point and the purpose or purposes for which we live and die and move through the universe are ever evolving. That's what I now believe. That belief is part of who I am and where I've come from. Part of my truth.

In time the "work" Maxine spoke of would be revealed to me. Everything she said that night, as best I can remember it, has come to pass. As I have followed the leadership of what I perceive to be God's Spirit in the myriad ways that he has chosen and chooses to speak to me and perhaps, through me, I have learned that I am very important to God. And I have learned, most importantly, that YOU ARE, too!

I am not different from you. We are all special in that grand and eternal scheme of things. I believe that God, whatever we perceive Him to be, well... He loves us, as we are and where we are. At any point in time, He is near to help us make sense of life or just ride it out as the call may be. And always He is near and willing to celebrate with us our uniqueness. He's proud of us. He longs to be friends with us. We are special. Of that I am CERTAIN.

I have become convinced that all true happiness this life offers comes from actively living out those three commandments that Jesus described to the inquisitive young lawyer 2000 years ago – the lawyer who demanded to know which "one" commandment was the greatest. It's all about relationships. Sharing ourselves with God and others is where it's at!

To do that well, to tap into the endless flow of peace and joy that is ours for the claiming, we must begin to know who we are and who He is. When that knowing gets underway, then the loving begins. And life is in the loving. Not just this life. But past life and all future life. All life! It's all in the knowing and the loving.

Psalm 91 means a great deal to me – the whole Psalm, but especially these few verses (As I understand it, this is God talking...):

"Because he has loved Me, therefore I will deliver him; I will set him securely on high, because he has known my name..."

And in another of the Psalms (139, specifically) I have read:
"Oh, Lord, Thou hast searched me and known me, Thou knowest when I sit down and when I rise up, Thou dost understand my thought from afar, Thou dost scrutinize my path, and my lying down and art intimately acquainted with all my ways..."

And it goes on and on and gets even more beautiful, and I believe those words. I know God knows me and loves me – just like I am. I'm telling you folks, there's energizing power in such knowing.

Years ago, just prior to the start of all the fall television premiers, I walked through the living room while my hubby was watching TV and caught a commercial blurb advertising an upcoming new show. I don't remember what the name of the show was, but it appeared that the main character was speaking and that she was standing in some kind of lab or morgue, and this is what she said as I walked through:
"The people that I see in the morning didn't know they were going to die last night."

What an attention getter, a real thought provoker! I loved that line... Stopped right then and there and wrote it down! I wish I could credit the author, but I don't know who he or she or they were. I believe that most folks believe in a hereafter – a life of sorts, for better or worse... beyond this realm. I do, for sure. But thankfully, believing that does not erase my need to be the best me I can be in this realm. Over the years, I really have grown to be deeply appreciative of any reminder that my time here could end any day. Are there better thoughts which can make you tune in faster to what you are doing with your life – how you are living it – what kind of impact you are having – what a difference you are making?

What could be a better attention getter than a comment like: "The people that I see in the morning didn't know they were going to die last night"? A statement like that can quickly drive home the importance of maintaining an eternally PRESENT state of mind and awareness of PURPOSE.

I once was asked if I personally coined the phrase: "eternally PRESENT state of mind." Probably not. I know I like it, have used it since my youth, and I encourage you to think on it. I like trying to live fully, completely, and with total awareness in the PRESENT moment, and doing it in a way that continues to prepare me to live happily and productively forever, while constantly gleaning wisdom from past experiences. Got that?

For the purposes of this book TODAY, and specifically regarding where I come from and who I am, I suppose there are thousands of stories I could tell you about people and circumstances that have influenced my life. I thought, at first that it would be hard to choose from among those people and circumstances. I was wrong. The one I just told you about Maxine rules, but before I move on, I think I do want to share a little more.

As this book began to take on an identity of its own, I realized there were many directions I could look in as I tried to discern how to best tell you about who I am and where I come from and I recalled a book convention I attended in Los Angeles, in 1999. I was walking around the exhibit floor, looking at new books, meeting new people, authors/publishers, the like... when I happened upon the Waldman House exhibit.

As I looked over their products, I discovered a little book called "The Next Place." I picked it up and began to read page after page, word for word. The tears welled up inside me. Tears that were left over from dozens of deaths, countless times when I had said goodbye to a friend, a relative, a patient. I was deeply moved. I was translated almost into another state of mind, another world, another somewhere that I had needed to go for a long time and that little book allowed me to go there while standing on the exhibit floor.

That day in L.A. as I finished the book, I suddenly noticed there were folks standing around me. Observing me. Curious as to what had so moved me.

One young whippersnapper, in his early 30's – I would say, and a marketing person with another publisher, asked to see what I was reading. He said he had to look at what could so affect me, just out of the blue like that. He glanced through the book. Did NOT drink it in – just glanced through the book. Made a few comments about how hard it was to follow the words that are literally and somewhat randomly thrown all over the page, which was one of the most effective things about the little book as far as I was concerned.

Now bear in mind, as he did this, and God knows he was entitled, I was still in a very strangely affected state of mind. Anyway… I politely, or maybe not so politely, reached out and took the book from him. Just took it out of his hands as though it was a treasure for which he was showing absolutely no respect. Snatched it back I did! Once I had rescued the book, I asked him had he ever lost anybody?

"What do you mean?" was his response.

"I mean" (I said with measured breath and through

almost clenched teeth), "Has anybody – close to you – ever died? Have you – through death – ever lost anyone you loved?"

"Well, no, not anybody close to me."

"Then forget about this book for now. But when that first loss happens, and the second, and third, and those that will follow, then you come back and read this book again. Your perception of this little book will change then." That is what I said to my far too self-confident, innocent, naïve, and probably very well meaning young 30-something whippersnapper!

Then I turned away from him to bask in the joy of my special moment and my discovery of something concrete that I could hold in my hand, close to my heart, right there on that crowded exhibit floor, something that assured me that somebody somewhere understood what some deep down inside part of me needed somebody to understand.

Now, you may be like that man. And if you are, I will be nicer to you today than I was to him. I have developed a tad more tact since then and experienced more personal healing. Thanks in part to the little book, "The Next Place," which I still cherish.

You see, I witnessed my first death when I was two

years old. I am very thankful today for that experience, because it occurred while I was cradled in the bosom of my mama's family. Right in the living room of my Aunt Grace's home, her son, William, nine years old, and one of my many first cousins, lay dying with leukemia.

And the family had gathered!

I try to say that with great emphasis because there is just no other way to say it. There was food spread out on a big table and lots of folks hugging and talking and crying and just being together. That's the day I began to learn that Gathered Families can get through anything together. The more widely spread out they are, and the more effort it takes to gather together, then the more the benefit is from the gathering! That's because they bring so much experience, wisdom and just plain long-standing love to the table.

AND the truth is, well it's a truth that the years have taught me – can't nobody put on a dyin' like my mama's family. It's a big family. A diverse family. Good guys. Bad guys. Lots of commonsense types. A few nuts and goons. I'm sure I have had every known label applied to me at one point in time or another – we all have. There is one thing, probably among many things, but one thing that has especially touched my life about this family. We are talking hundreds of first, second and third cousins who have emerged from the households of ten brothers and sisters. Among this clan there is always somebody who will understand where you are coming from and what you are going through.

Maybe not exactly, but pretty darn close.

And whoever that somebody is, – they will know whether or not to call in back-up. And when a dying's going down, back-up gets called in. Big time!

You share. You laugh. You cry. You remember. You cherish. You regret. You plan ahead. You let go. And you can do it all when you let yourself be held in the bosom of this family. That has been my heritage. I have been extraordinarily blessed. I wouldn't trade it for the world. I would clone it all if I could, and share it, but I can't.

I can only take to an occasional podium now and then, write stories and books, and host radio programs in an effort to share some of the life lessons that my family, friends and experiences have taught me over time. I enjoyed including in my "You Are Somebody and I am, too" book of stories, back in 2004, a narrative about my mama's family and my southern roots and how a really good dyin' celebration unfolds! I will share it with you here.

My Mama's Family – April 2002

"Would you like anything from the buffet while I'm up?"

"Yes, I'd like a piece of that chocolate cake."

"There's only one slice left."

"I'll take it," Betty said.

Gasps went up around the room.

"I know! Mama always told me not to take the last piece of anything, but along about the time I turned 50, I started taking the last piece of anything I wanted."

Laughter rang out in the extended dining area. Most folks in that never to be forgotten setting identified. I, who have been eating dessert FIRST for years, saw much wisdom in the revelation that had been laid out before us.

I suspect there are, in all families, never to be forgotten moments packed with extraordinary tidbits of wisdom, joy, peace and comfort. Moments we hold to our breast, deep in the corners of our hearts, for times when we no longer are surrounded by those we love and those who love us.

I am most blessed. No one who has come before me, or who will follow after me, can ever know more joy than I have known in more ways than I can count. It is awkward to make that claim, knowing how much pain and suffering there is in the world. It is my claim, however, and I make it reverently.

You see, I come from a really big family and family is where it's at! There is no end to what "it" can teach you. The varieties of ways in which "it" can sustain you, restore you, fortify you, and empower you also are endless.

It is said that we all may be subject to fifteen minutes of fame sooner or later. I don't know about that, but if I ever did make any claim to fame, I would want that claim to somehow revolve around my having been born out of this crazy, wonderful extended family.

That's real important because some families keep you aware that you can always go home again. And going home again should not be taken lightly.

It is not to be confused with knowing where you've come from. That's important, too. It helps you to get where you are going. But to actually be able to go home again is a rare and precious thing.

THOSE MOMENTS THAT MATTER

I went home yet again this past weekend to celebrate Aunt Benonia's passing. My family does not just bury folks. A funeral is really only incidental to the way we celebrate the exit our loved ones make from the bodies they live in while on earth, although the funerals are indeed something to talk about!

Aunt Benonia is the one who – due to a long, long illness – had experienced more "dyings" than any other family member amongst my clan.

It was on April 17 that she finally left this earth. Well.... actually, she may not have left until after the service. She wanted really bad to hang around for it, and if there was any way possible, I'm sure she did. What's more, I'm sure she enjoyed it! I know I did. Don't think I've ever enjoyed anybody's dying celebration quite so much.

There are the throngs of friends and relatives that come and go. There's an endless supply of food and drink brought in by friends and neighbors. The children quickly and easily figure out how to entertain themselves.

Hugs, laughter, tears abound. Memories rule. They carry you. They sustain you. They become you. Thus, the never-ending cycle of life goes on. And in that weak moment when the memories are blurred and you can't quite feel that hug you need so much, then it's okay if you want to go for the last piece of chocolate cake. Ain't no mama, dead or alive, gonna slap your hand 'cause they've been there, too.

I share this story and others to tell you, without a doubt, it has been the deaths that have most influenced my life. The dying have taught me to live. In large families it seems like there's almost never a year that passes that you don't lose somebody you loved or somebody who has loved you.

You lose.

You let go.

You learn and you move on.

CHAPTER TWENTY-TWO

To not move on would be the most gosh awful sign of disrespect you could ever show to those who have left you behind to carry on. A great deal of dying outside my family has touched my life as well. Though I never really dreamed of or even planned to be a nurse, I found myself entering nursing school right out of high school.

When we started clinicals, one of my professors assigned me to a 30-year-old woman who had terminal cancer. Ovarian. I grew close to her. Very. I think that relationship years ago is one of many reasons, recording artist Joey Feek's cancer battle and death affected me so deeply. For several months, in 1966 and 67, each time the woman would be readmitted to the hospital my professor would reassign me to her, or her to me. I was never quite sure just how that worked.

I reached the point where I went to my teacher in tears begging to be taken off the case. I was denied. That wise teacher squarely looked me in the eye and said, "It is clear to me that you have certain unique gifts, and I am doing my part to see that you develop them."

Some part of me, on some level, hated her for that. Then. But not the day I attended my 32-year-old patient's funeral. And not today, because I came to realize there was indeed "a gift." In the somewhat forced development of the gift, which I did not appreciate at all at the time, I have become a very wealthy woman. Wealthy in experience. Wealthy in fortitude. Wealthy in understanding. Wealthy spiritually. Wealthy in so many ways. Not much money to show for it, but that may be the part that is most valuable – learning that money ain't all some folks make it out to be.

There is no way to measure all the wisdom and wealth that first patient shared with me in the last 24 months of her life, because the gift my nursing instructor observed, and did her part to develop, has taken me into the hearts and lives of countless "dying" individuals who have taught me more about living than I ever would have imagined I could learn!

Granted, we are all dying from the day we are born. I know that on some level, and so do you. But those who are given a label of "terminally ill" experience that truth on an entirely different level of awareness. I have been invited many times by special people to visit with them in those deeply spiritual realms where truth rules. When I have lingered there with them, I often have glimpsed that which really matters in life. I have been taught life lessons that only death can teach, and I would not trade those lessons for anything in this world.

Such experiences, however, may have led to an extreme sensitivity to death. If the truth be told… maybe it was the sensitivity that led to the experiences. Regardless of what came first, a personal sensitivity to death and dying, or vice versa, in 1986, it all got to me. Took a big toll. I chose then to leave the clinical nursing setting for a while in pursuit of another way or ways to heal.

But first I had to find healing for me…

Several deaths in the early 80's hurt so much that I did not know any way to cope except with and through my pen and paper – a pen and paper that my mom had first put in my hands as a young preschool child in an effort to help calm me when I would be gasping for breath while in the grasp of an acute asthma attack, or flighting claustrophobia in one of those old fashioned oxygen tents.

Knowing what I must do to heal me, I picked up that pen and began to use it, I hope wisely. For the most part, my pen has served me well. The poems, the stories, the recorded random thoughts have been therapeutic. Throughout my life, as they have flowed out of me and onto paper, I have been healed. Again and again. With each stage of healing, I have grown stronger. Wiser. More free. More open to being me in all the ways I was born to freely be me.

Perhaps it was simply part of the natural order of my life for a very wise Dr. Hayes W. Wilson to encourage me in 2003 to try to write away the harmful emotional aftermath of a serious illness from which I was recovering at the time. The result of that therapeutic writing will be published under the title "Dear Doctor, I am your teacher."

I've been told that golf does it for some people, or tennis or even gardening. It is writing, however, that always has had a very healing effect on me, but there are many other things that I do to keep myself growing and continuously becoming. I surround myself with uplifting music, books, art, poetry and people. I make an ongoing effort to keep a circle of honest, but positive thinking folks in my life. Oh, and it is never too early to start assembling a collection of uplifting and funny movies.

Talk about therapy! I must laugh sometimes. I have to do that. Sometimes laughter is not only the best medicine, but the only medicine. I choose to be aware of and try to avoid ugliness, and horror, and mean-spirited people, both in person and in film. I love that little song that we kids were taught in the southern churches of my childhood:

"Oh, be careful little eyes what you see
  Oh, be careful little ears what you hear
    Oh, be careful little feet where you go."

What wisdom there was in those lyrics! I try to educate myself regarding everything good and bad that affects me. I try to cover all bases! If I anticipate a thing – any ... thing – good or bad, that could have a life-changing impact on me, then I try to imagine every kind of way it might unfold ... every kind of response I might offer to it. I think things through in an active, preparatory kind of way and that often requires evaluating the negatives. But I almost always, in the end, choose to THINK ON the good stuff.

I can choose to look for and dwell stagnantly among negativity, pain, misery and anxiety. I can claim every label I can imagine that might get me sympathy or a "break." ... or I can look for the positive up-lifting forward-moving good stuff, put my focus there, and CHOOSE to move towards the future with confidence as I build on a solid foundation of true, honorable, right, pure, lovely things. I can choose excellence. I can choose to be thankful. I can choose to be happy. And, thankfully, for the most part that is what I do.

Oh, and I also like to pray – morning and night, wherever I am, and sometimes, in between, at an altar. An altar marks the spot where you talked to God... I cannot ever over emphasize the importance of an altar. Things happen there – the kinds of things about which you want to remember where and when.

What I'm sharing somewhat randomly on these pages is some degree of who I am, where I come from in part, and why I care about you. There's more, but I repeat, no factor so dominates my life like my awareness of how quickly death can come. I see that awareness as both a strength and a weakness, because it has been both for me.

It probably can be said of all of us that on occasion our greatest strengths have been our greatest weaknesses. It certainly can be said of me. For instance, a deep sensitivity to the needs of the dying often has led me to extend myself far beyond what I was physically and emotionally capable of being extended. Nothing, absolutely nothing, is more exhausting than to try to love on and support a dying person whose life is riddled with regret over things NOT done. All of us mess up. Oh, yeah, we blow it! We get it wrong and start over again and again. But the regret that constantly reminds us of what we never even tried to do is almost unbearable.

Know with me that a strength wisely used brings great rewards. Unwisely used, it can backfire in myriad ways.

One more very important thing – I have absolutely no fear now of being called contradictory. In fact, over time I have almost come to the point of considering such a description a compliment! Because what I might think, feel, or say regarding one issue or happenstance TODAY, may not be at all what I would think or say tomorrow about a similar issue or happening. I think the most accurate compliment my husband ever paid me was when he said the only consistent thing about me is my inconsistency. I figure that abiding attribute shows I am open and growing, not stuck and stale.

We are all in this thing called life together. Yep! So, as long as I am breathing, and experiencing, and hopefully learning from my life experiences, then my opinion, views, thoughts, etc. will ever be evolving. I trust that I always will be changing. Always becoming. The dying have taught me that right up until our last earthly breath, and perhaps even beyond… we are always becoming.

My faith, or absence thereof at times, also has greatly influenced who I am and helped me to know that I am somebody special, and that I'm worth my making the effort to know and love me. Every major religion, to some degree, teaches respect for self and others. Every single one teaches: Self love. Self respect. Self knowledge.

Who I am and where I come from tells me these things matter. Big time! A "poor me" – "I'm so unworthy" – "I don't know why God would love me, but He does" kind of attitude, or thinking, or talking does not set well with me. Though I have learned to try to be somewhat tolerant of those with that mindset; I have after all, been there myself a time or two, but I didn't like it, so I didn't stay there!

I have personally come to believe that I'm God's kid and you are, too. I am convinced that we are special and unique creations. I know that life's unfavorable influences and bad choices can take a person of great beauty and awesome potential and make him look like garbage, but I choose to believe that always there is within that person the innate potential to become something more, something better, someone who can know his or her God, who can walk and talk with that God, who can hear in the depths of his heart the voice of that God calling him by NAME.

Now that I finally hear it, I personally would not trade being able to hear what I perceive to be that voice for all the world – THAT voice helps me to know I am somebody special. The ability to hear it may now rule the essence of who I am.

CHAPTER TWENTY-THREE

He was the love of my life, a life laced with a million moments that mattered much over five decades. Our first moment of live interaction occurred on December 13, 1967. I had just graduated from nursing school, was in a most celebratory mood, and was out riding on the back of a fire engine with a fellow student and two Marines who were our dates. It was a lovely and exciting night, twinkling with Christmas decorations everywhere, when suddenly I had to tinkle. I had also had my first mixed drink ever a little earlier! I asked the firefighter to stop in front of my friend's apartment so I could run in for a moment.

He did and I did. And there Daniel sat on my friend's sofa. He was wearing white jeans, and I think it was a blue shirt. The sleeves were turned up in a James Dean fold that highlighted his so very well-defined biceps. It was lust at first sight. I was wearing a red suit and heels. Skirt was above the knee, but not a mini. Later, he told me it was love at first sight for him. I think my friend officially introduced us, although I have no idea what was said. I do recall sitting on the arm of a chair for a couple of minutes, and trying to drink in his gorgeousness, and crossing my long legs just so…! Then out the door I went.

A few weeks later, on Monday after Christmas, I was visiting that same friend before going to work, a night shift, at the local hospital. The doorbell rang. She asked me to go downstairs and let him in. I did, and that is when it happened. I saw his eyes. The eyes at the top of that extraordinary body. I recognized them. I had dreamed of them when I was five years old. My mom and dad and brother and I had spent the night with my maternal grandparents, in the tiniest little house ever, and we had all slept in the tiniest little full-sized bed ever. That morning when I awakened, I told my mother I had dreamed about the man I would marry. "What did he look like?" she asked. "I don't know. I only saw his eyes, but they were beautiful, sort of blue and green," I said.

Looking back, I am glad the vision was only of his eyes. Can you imagine the hormonal misery I would have had to endure during my teens if the whole package had been part of my foreknowledge of the man standing before me that night?

So there I was at the foot of the stairs, and there he stood with those eyes. LordyMercy! Could not be! I was not ready. I had just graduated from nursing school. I did not even have my license yet. Was planning to work my way through journalism school. Long story. I will try to make it short. We were poor. Not well to do at all. No money for college. Not a penny. My grades were not good enough for a scholarship. I was the oldest of seven kids, had always been quite sickly, and our family doctor had taken an interest in me. He knew I wanted to be a journalist and that I wanted to someday write books, but he thought I had a gift for healing.

Since the kind of education I wanted was beyond my reach, he suggested I let him get me on at the local hospital as a Nurse's Aide right after graduation. "If you like it and I think you will, then maybe we can get you hooked up with Vocational Rehabilitation and see if they will pay for you to attend technical school and get your LPN. That way you can work your way through college and study whatever you like." Yep, that was what he said, and the good doctor made it happen. I was well on my way to my dream when there at the foot of those stairs stood an extraordinary hunk of a man who was about to throw a huge monkey wrench into my plans. He followed me upstairs and the three of us visited for a while before I had to leave for work. At one point when my friend (his date) went to the kitchen to stir the spaghetti sauce he asked me out for the following Friday night. I said, "Sure!"

The next morning when I arrived home from work my mom met me on the back porch with her broom. She had just hung wet laundry on the clothesline to dry and the neighbor's dogs were playing under it. She threw me the broom and told me to go chase away the dogs. I did, but I ran into the clothesline and fell backwards on the broom handle. Got a pretty nice goose egg on the back of my head but ignored it. Went to bed. Slept all day. My mother had to wake me. That night around 2 a.m. when my supervisor came around for the nightly report, I had trouble talking. I told her that I had a bad headache and she checked out the knot on my head. In short order I got admitted with a concussion. Later that morning I asked my mother to call Daniel and cancel my date with him. She did, but he showed up at the hospital that night and on Wednesday, too. He came again on Thursday night and that's when he proposed. Sure enough. Asked me to marry him before he ever even kissed me. I said "yes, but… I will not say obey in my vows and I will never love you more than God." He said, "Fine, but I like to hunt every fall and that might come first then."

After I said I would marry him, then he kissed me. Aiyiyi! Yep, AND . THEN . HE . KISSED . ME with those lips that were just below those beautiful eyes. On Monday, four days later, he went back to Vietnam. He mailed me an engagement ring for Valentine's Day. My sister put it on my finger.

He came back home on May 19. Called me when he landed in Seattle. Asked me to go get his car from his mom's house, a new blue Malibu; he'd bought it when he was home on leave. Stick shift. I drove an automatic. The night got interesting. I was wearing white jeans and a pink tank top. I had five bucks for gas. Yep, I was broke after I used that to fill the tank, and back then it did actually fill the tank! I'd never been north of Macon, but I set out for the Atlanta airport. I arrived at that magnificent terminal around 3 a.m. It was back when there was this amazing round rotunda through which travelers from all over the world passed. It would have been people watching heaven for this country girl if I had not had to tinkle so badly. All the doors in the bathroom had locks that required a dime to open them. My bladder was truly about to pop when he walked off the plane. I held out my hand and said, "I need a dime." He gave it to me. I used the dime, then I went back and hugged and kissed him. It wasn't much of kiss because he said he needed to brush his teeth. Once we were headed back south, he pulled over, bought a toothbrush and toothpaste, used them, then oh, my!

My!My!My!

No, we did not have sex then. Just kisses. Great, magical kisses. The following Sunday night he came to my apartment. Yep, the same one in which I had first met him. My friend had moved away, and I lived there then. We sat on the sofa and watched and listened to Billy Graham preach a sermon about sex. Not so much about having sex or how to have sex, just about when it was right to do it. I promise you he did not say it was right or appropriate for us to have sex that night, but, oh, well. When the last amen was said, Daniel looked at me and said, "Want to go to the bedroom?" I said, "Yes." It was awful. It was nothing like I had imagined. It was fast and furious and over quickly. In the coming years, I would come to like it like that, even prefer it that way sometimes. But that night, it was just awful.

A few weeks later, on June 13, we set out on a journey in which Daniel would make it up to me. We told everybody we were going to Atlanta to visit his Uncle Bill. He called Uncle Bill and asked him to cover for us. Then we went to Montgomery, AL, for the most amazing ever 48 hours or so of sex. I much prefer to believe my firstborn son was conceived during our wild weekend in Montgomery, but I know better. Billy Graham had set the stage for that conception nearly four weeks earlier. Sexually, nothing every quite topped those approximately 3000 moments that mattered so much that weekend in Montgomery, but it was not for a lack of trying over the years to come! We did take a break at one point to go see "Gone with the Wind." Other than that, well… that weekend of sin was gloriously magnificent.

Then Sunday morning came, and I started crying. Of course, I did not know at that point that I was already pregnant from the quick sperm deposit a few weeks earlier and that my hormones were already flipping out. I thought it was my Baptist upbringing. When Daniel asked why I was crying I told him I felt bad about lying. And I did. You know what he did? He called Uncle Bill and told him we had to come see him. He then drove us from Montgomery to north Atlanta, then back to Albany, GA so I could rest easy that I had not lied about going to see Uncle Bill.

CHAPTER TWENTY-FOUR

For a number of reasons, I had taken that engagement ring off my finger about a month before Daniel returned home. I had even stopped writing to him. My sister took it upon herself to write in my place so certain she was that he was my intended. But I was having doubts. For one thing, I had met his family. His sister-in-law, at our first meeting, had made a comment which led me to believe I had no idea what I was doing getting engaged to Daniel. She observed quite assertively that he and I were total opposites, leading me to believe that he was a drinking, fighting, womanizing party animal. In time I would learn that her observations were indeed dead on. Absolutely correct. Before he met me.

Regardless of all that, when he called me from Seattle and asked me to meet him in Atlanta, I melted at the sound of his voice. So, although I was not wearing his ring, I still drove to meet him and the attraction was still overwhelmingly strong, even stronger that I had imagined it might be, and, trust me, I had imagined much! I gave the ring back to him and told him we had to get to know one another better first. Oh, we talked and played and visited family and friends, but the truth is we mostly got to know one another's bodies in the coming days and short weeks. It would be more than 20 years before we came to a comfortable knowing of the minds. In no time at all, I again was growing sure that he was indeed the man for me.

Those eyes… there was just no denying those eyes and all that came with them! So he was going to give the ring back to me for my birthday. Planned to put it on my finger himself this time. But a few weeks before my July birthday I finally realized I was pregnant. Actually, my sister, who was five years younger, figured it out. I was moody. I was crying a lot. And yes, I had missed a couple of menstrual cycles, but that was not uncommon. I was sickly and on a lot of meds for asthma and allergies and those medications took a toll. So I saw a gynecologist. He confirmed my sister's suspicions. Therefore, no way was I going to marry. Nope. Not hardly! It was 1960 something and back then it was said that women who married after getting pregnant did so because they "had to."

Daniel tried to give me the ring back before my birthday. I said no and told him that I could not marry him "because I was pregnant" and there was no way I was going to marry a man because I "had to do so." Oh, my! That so totally did not go over well! Never did a man argue so much and fight so hard for a woman and a child.

Eventually, on my birthday I did let him slip that

beautiful ring back on my finger. We got married a month later and set out for Tulsa, Oklahoma so he could go to school and get his Airframe and Powerplant License. He had been a sheet metal mechanic for four years in the Air Force and had served 22 months of that time in Vietnam, with boots on the ground. He definitely had PTSD when he returned, but back then it did not have a well-recognized label, and soldiers returning from that war were not welcomed, or honored, or even recognized as having issues that might have life altering consequences.

We did not last long in Tulsa. I stayed sick and cried a lot. His sister called one day and told him that Delta Airlines was hiring mechanics based on their military, especially Vietnam, experience. He decided we needed to come back to Georgia. We packed our meager belongings in a little trailer and hooked it to the back of that blue Malibu and headed home. When we stopped for gas, he asked me for the money. We had 72 dollars when we left Tulsa. I had packed it in a metal trunk he had built. I am still not sure exactly how that happened. That trunk was under all our other belongings in that trailer. He had to unload the whole thing to access our money and pay for the gas. He did it without fussing one bit. He knew I would cry. I never had morning sickness. No vomiting at all, but I sure did some crying during that pregnancy!

Delta hired him in early December. We moved into an apartment in Riverdale, GA. We were country kids, and it was misery, but we managed. Our friends, Judy and Perry, came to visit occasionally and Perry always bought juicy red steaks, massive potatoes for baking, salad makings and all the trimmings. We were so broke that we truly rejoiced when they visited. Occasionally we would walk up and down the road and pick up coke (soda, if you are not from the south) bottles, sell them for three cents each, and go to the Dairy Queen for treats. I really could not cook worth a lick. I was awful. But I had this wonderful Dinner for Two Cookbook from Betty Crocker and I could follow directions. One week I splurged, bought two green bell peppers and stuffed them with a meat mixture in which I put way too much salt, but he ate them. He talked later and often of that salt… but not while he was eating, not once did he complain. He was not a complainer. Not ever. The peppers just became a story. One of many in which we packed a lot of moments that mattered.

Our son was born in February and Daniel wanted him to have his name, so Daniel Dean Holt, Jr. it was! After Dean was born, we started looking for something more rural. By the end of 1969 we were living in a little four room rental in Fayette County,

Georgia, with a big yard and nice garden spot where we grew the biggest tomatoes I had ever seen. Still today I have never seen any bigger that those. They were Rutgers and that variety does not normally grow big like that, but those did! They were wonderful!

During the summer of 1970, my brother came to spend the summer with us and babysit, so I worked part time to help save enough money for a three acre lot we had discovered was for sale only about three miles from where we were renting. Delightfully, it was on a dusty dirt road. Sadly, the road got paved right after we bought the land. We built a 1200 square foot ranch with a full basement, moved into it in December 1971, and lived there for 28 years. Yep, truly lived! Oscar Wilde had it right, "To live is the rarest thing in the world; most people just exist." Not us. We lived!

When we decided we were ready for baby number two, we already knew how fertile I was so we were just waiting for the twinge that comes with ovulation and decide to have sex wherever we were when I felt it. Remember the uncle in Atlanta? Well, we were visiting him when it happened. I felt it. I winked at him. We went to the bathroom together, had a fabulous quickie and that did the trick! I panicked a few days later thinking we were not financially comfortable enough yet and started back on my birth control pills, but it was too late. Derrick D'Wayne, the sweetest, most caring little human ever was already on his way! He was born shortly after midnight on Easter Sunday morning in 1971.

Later that year, I got arrested for stealing, specifically shoplifting. I only had money to buy one coat, so I stole two others for my three younger sisters because my dad had called me and told me they did not have coats for the winter. He did not have the money to buy them. He asked me to check at Goodwill. I did. Nothing was there. So I tried to get them by stealing. It is strange what we will do for family. It happened on Daniel's birthday. All that he revealed about himself through that ordeal made me know I had married a priceless jewel.

There are so many things I could share about our life together, our sons, their loves, their lives, our extended family, and the best friends on earth, but I do not want to. Not now. Maybe another time…

I think it is time to think about closing this attempt at a memoir of sorts in my somewhat feeble effort to remind us all that the moments that matter are fleeting and we must live them well.

It is as I wrote earlier, 2020. What a year! I'm still alive. My husband is not. I am sad. I am looking at a magnificent black and silver urn across the room that held his ashes for a while until I could bring myself to scatter them as he requested. His niece and nephew did it for me in a field they helped him clear of rocks so it could become a food plot for his beloved wildlife. At this writing, there is a worn and yellowed piece of notebook paper laying in a basket near the urn. That basket contains notes and cards to which I still have not responded since Daniel's death. Also, in the basket is a newspaper section containing his obituary. One day, not too long after Daniel's death, amidst my ultimate breakdown week from hell, or heaven one, not sure which, but that's okay, God's still God and life, as it is presently unfolding on earth is still life ... anyway, during that horrible meltdown, I walked over to the table on which the urn and basket set at the time, and I saw that piece of paper sticking out. It did not belong. I picked it up and read it. I was and still am shocked.

I recognized it immediately.

A long time ago, there had been a wrongful death (medical malpractice) at an area hospital. He was my absolute favorite patient (yes, healthcare professionals have favorites) at the medical office where I worked. He was a retired but gifted engineer, a bridge builder, a planter of flowers, a Bible scholar... and my friend. His horrific death was so painful for me that it became a major influence in my decision to leave nursing and see if I could do more to heal and help the truly weak and vulnerable with pen and ink.

After he died, I had struggled long with my grief and anger, when one morning while washing dishes, I had the radio on and I heard Dr. Charles Stanley say, *"Here's what you could have done if you had been willing to let go of all the hurts, regrets and bitterness. The spirit that conquers is able to forget in order to forge ahead in God's love."* I dried my hands and quickly wrote those words down on the piece of yellowed paper laying on top of the basket in front of me. I have no idea how it got into that basket. I have wondered long. The only thing I can figure is it might have been in some of the photo and memento boxes we went through after Daniel died and someone thought it should go in that basket of cards and messages, tucked into the newspaper containing Daniel's obituary.
"Someone..." Yeah, "someone" reminded me that day:
"Here's what you could have done if you had been willing to let go of all the hurts, regrets and bitterness. The spirit that conquers is able to forget in order to forge ahead in God's love."

CHAPTER TWENTY-FIVE

Before I attempt to end this memoir, I need to share a little basic history... In 1986, on Labor Day weekend, I was at the city auditorium in Thomasville, Georgia for the annual "All Night Gospel Singing." There, I had the first of three visions that prompted me to take the road which has led to where I am today. Visions were something I only had read about in the Bible until that night. I do not think I really believed in visions until then. I'd had my share of dreams while I was sleeping, dreams that later came true. I had grown used to them, but visions were something else. There was no dismissing my first vision. In the midst of the music and a tremendous air of celebration, with my sister sitting to my right and strangers all around, suddenly I saw a hologram of a miniature wagon train on the stage circling The Galileans, from Texas, as they sang. Just like in an old western movie, the little wagon train was being called to a halt and instructed to make a circle for the evening. It was a split-second kind of eternal thing.

I do not know how the experience manifested itself on my countenance, but my sister asked what was wrong. It was so vivid for me that I asked if she could see it too. She said no. She watched me rather closely for the rest of the evening. I decided then that my wagon train was not something I ought to tell folks about any time soon. If she had trouble believing, and she was right there beside me, what would the rest of the world think?

The following Sunday night, after the evening worship service, I went to the altar of my home church to prayerfully discuss with God the strange occurrence I could not easily dismiss.

While kneeling there pouring out my heart, asking what it meant, if anything, I had my second vision! It does not remain so vivid today as the first and third, but as I recall, in it the wagon master told everybody to prepare to rest for a few days, not just overnight. I think it was also this second vision where I realized I was part of the wagon train.

The next Sunday evening I returned to that same spot at the altar for session three. I knew it would come. It came. It was disturbing. It changed my life.

Again, immediately upon starting to pray, I saw the wagon train. This time the wagon master told everybody to hitch up their teams and prepare to move out (again, just like in the movies!) — everybody but me. He told me to unload everything from my wagon and set my animals free.

I protested, "But how will I cross the mountains?"

"Take my hand and I will lead," he said, "we are

going to walk together across the mountains."

...For two years prior to this series of visions, I had felt "called" (another word I had a hard time with until it happened to me) to pursue the interests and professions I now enjoy so much. On Monday morning, following the third vision, I turned in my resignation at the family practice office where I had worked for six years. It was hard to leave a staff and patients who were like family, to give up an identity with which I had been safe and comfortable for eighteen years. It was hard, but to have stayed would have been harder because I had mountains to climb and a Personal Guide was waiting. The best was yet to come.

I spent the last two weeks of September 1986, and the first two weeks of October walking and praying in the woods behind my home. When I would come inside, I would write. It was during those four weeks that I wrote my first book, "From the Corners of my Heart." In late October I went to the local paper and asked the general manager if I could write a column for his newspaper that was about to celebrate its 100th year of publication. He told me he did not need another columnist and asked me to leave. As I reached for the handle to my car door out in the parking lot, that manager opened the front door and called to me. He asked if I could really write.

"Of course I can write," I answered.

"Well the woman who does my church and school news is about to be out for three months having a baby. You can fill in for her," he said.

"I don't want a job. I want a column," I answered.

"Take it or leave it," he responded.

"Can I have a column if I take the job?" I asked.

"Yes, you can have a column," he said.

And so it began.

When it came time for the lady to come back to her job, the manager asked me if I would stay on. I said yes. At that point I was given the title of Religion Editor as well as three pages in the Saturday paper to fill with church news each week.

I did not even know how to type yet, but I already had borrowed a typing manual from Connie Brezina who homeschooled her sons and I was learning. I bought other teaching aids and started to educate myself for the mountains that lay ahead.

The following year and the year after that my column won first place in the Georgia Press Association Inspirational Writing category. After that, I never entered it again and I would not allow my editors to do so. I did not like thinking about writing for awards. I wanted to write for the people. For the grandma who clipped my column and mailed it to her granddaughter out of state. For the bankteller who cut it out and placed it on the front of her refrigerator. For the high school English teacher who used it to teach creative writing to her students. THAT is how I measured my success then, and I still measure it that way today. I have refused numerous nominations for various awards. It takes something away from what I do. People tell me awards can open doors. I tell them I am good with God opening the doors through which I need to walk. He has supplied my every need as I have walked in obedience to him.

Obedience has not been easy, however. Jump forward from 1986 to 2011. Pears. I was still writing my column and had written a few books. I had published a magazine from 1988 until 2000. I had enjoyed helping others get their stories told as an editor and sometimes by custom publishing projects for clients. The year before, I had helped a friend get started in broadcasting, then walked away. All the while he was telling me that I was the one who should be in broadcasting, not him. To this day it is hard for me to admit he was right. It is a pride thing. But that turned out to be a most miserable year. As it turns out, he was dead on and I was pridefully, even arrogantly disobedient.

God is a God of second chances, however – many second chances. In early spring the following year, my husband and I were pruning our pear trees. We took a break and drove to a nearby convenience store for an ice cream. The manager of a local radio/television station was there doing a live remote. We chatted. He asked me if I would be willing to host the local "about town" television program. They needed to replace the lady who had been hosting it.

My answer was not no, but hell no. I had turned down a number of offers to "do television" over the years. It did not interest me. So, I countered with, "But I will host a radio program for you."

"We don't need that" he said, "I need a television talk show host to interview local guests."

"Not me," I responded.

He called me the following Monday and asked if I would reconsider. I said "I will do the TV thing if you will give me a radio spot."

It was THAT Monday that Tommy Brandt stopped by in his tour bus for a brief visit. Shortly after he arrived, several cancellations happened. He stayed parked at my farm for six weeks and helped me set up my home recording studio. He also was my first guest on the television program I had to host for three months. They canceled it at that point because a deal to buy several other stations fell through.

The manager at that station "gave" me an hour on Sunday mornings for my radio program, "Corner of Country with MJ." Then a second hour on Sunday nights to re-air it. Then two hours. Then three hours. I played Christian Country music and told stories about the artists and writers on that program. Hunter Logan at hleradio.com picked it up. A few years later I launched my "Reach to Touch" talk show and eventually stopped producing Corner of Country.

I mentioned earlier that I have prophetic dreams. Over the past few years, I have a had a series of such dreams about feeding people, dreams that seem to be tied to Christ's command, "If you love Me, feed my sheep."

Even before the dreams started, back when I facilitated my empowerment workshops, I always fed the attendees. I thought it was important then to do that. I know it is now. So, at the present time, I host a weekly bible study and I always feed those who attend. I don't want to screw up my orders to feed so I cook food and share when I can, study and share the Scriptures, write books, and speak from my heart about what I think are those moments that matter now and forever.

Many years ago, a fellow nursing student shared with me the following words which I recorded on a blank page separating the Old and New Testament in my oldest Bible. I regret I do not know the origin, or author, of these words which I now share with you:

"Once I fit together the bits, pieces, hopes, fears and desires that make me the person I am, I hope to have the courage to act on my discoveries and follow them through. The adventure will be well worth the quest. Once I find a pattern of life so absorbing that I lose myself in it, then I will find myself."

The adventure has proven well worth the quest. In losing myself have I found deeper faith, and with the Guide I have had, the mountains have been more like majestic rolling hills. I hope to share more in the future as the journey continues.

Like I said earlier, I have traveled this planet now for more than 70 years in my present, and at times fragile, 5'8" earth suit. Activity in this realm and others has led me to discover many truths. Among those revelations is an abiding awareness of the angels in our midst among the dancing demons on all the broad ways of our lives. I hope you are aware of them as your moments that matter so very much unfold. Such discernment is important.

Here is why wise discernment is important:

Matthew 7:13-14 (KJV)

Enter ye in at the strait gate: for wide is the gate, and broad is the way, that leadeth to destruction, and many there be which go in there at: Because strait is the gate, and narrow is the way, which leadeth unto life, and few there be that find it.

That passage from Matthew's Gospel, along with a reminder that there truly is much you can do if you are willing to let go of all the hurts, regrets and bitterness makes me know Dr. Stanley was correct, *"The spirit that conquers is able to forget in order to forge ahead in God's love."*

~~~

Please watch for upcoming volumes of:
- "SOUL FOOD and Spirit Vittles;"
- "Dear Doctor, I am your teacher…";
- an extraordinary self-empowerment book which will probably incorporate "YOU CHOOSE" into the title;
- a re-release of "What IS Love?"
- as well as a re-release of "Malignant Emotion;"
  and just possible a sequel to "Malignant Emotion" featuring our dear Vic. Like others, I truly love his character!

In closing...

Before I leave you, I must refer to something I said earlier about those Bible "Sword Drills" of my youth. Hebrews 4:12 is why they were called that, *"For the word of God is quick and powerful and sharper than any two edged sword, piercing even to the dividing asunder of soul and spirit, and of the joints and marrow, and is a discerner of the thoughts and intents of the heart."*

Back then, I had no idea how learning those passages would later impact my life – even save my life. I perceive Jesus Christ Himself to be THE Word of God. I know, however, that Jesus understood the power of the written and spoken Scriptures. What I did not say earlier is that there were a few weeks in my life, about three years after my neighbor's suicide and shortly after the automobile accident that left me in pain still today, when I could not think. I could barely go through the motions of living and I contemplated suicide often.

During that time, I would wake up every morning with weird words in my mind. Puzzling phrases. They did not seem applicable to what was happening at the time, what I now believe to have been all out spiritual warfare. It took a few days before I started to research the strange words or phrases. I found them to be biblical passages that I had first studied as a young girl during those "Sword Drills." Once I realized what was happening, I started printing them. At one point, I had those verses, and others I found when researching the phrase of the day, taped all over one wall of my bedroom. It was a wondrous time. A healing time. A time of discovery about the power of the written and spoken words of our Holy Scriptures.

I am glad you have read my memoir. I hope you will read my other books. However, if your time is limited and you must choose, go with the Holy Scriptures. Read and study them for yourself, but never let another person use them to try to manipulate you. They will try to do that because I promise you that Satan and all his demons know those Scriptures better than you or I ever will. They understand the power that is in them.

Do not be misled. Simply confess that you are unable to be all you have been born to be on your own, that you fall short… and express your belief in Jesus Christ, acknowledge your need for Him as Savior, Friend and even Lord, then ask His Holy Spirit to guide you in all things. It will. It will be the soft whisper you will hear in your heart of hearts, the one that waits to be heard over all the noise we let into our lives.

If I am leaving you uneasy, you may be able to remedy that uneasiness by reading the Fourth Gospel (Book of John), and then read Paul's letter to the Ephesians which you will find a little deeper into the New Testament. In this realm there will always be more questions than answers, but through Jesus Christ peace can be found. And joy… If I can find it, I would imagine that anybody can! Goodbye for now. More later.

Please visit the maryjaneholt.com website and use the link there to share your questions or answers with me. I would love to hear from you.

THOSE MOMENTS THAT MATTER

I WANT TO GO HOME
Mary Jane Holt

I want to go home
My eyes are swelling
They burn
I can barely see
My heart is aching
It hurts
I long to be free
From this pain inside
That stings
When I pause to think of them
From the hurts that hide
As part of a past
Now growing dim

My gaze looks upward
To One Who offers His Hand
And says,

"Walk forward
I am here
I shall help you to stand
Linger there no longer
There are mountains ahead
Get out of the valley
Let's start climbing instead"
The call through the hills came ringing

And started my heart to singing
For I knew the day would come
When I would understand
Why it was best
That things had not worked out
As I had planned
From heavenward

The voice came again,
"You must linger there no longer
Do not dare to think you will fail
You just think you need to be stronger
But you have a story to tell NOW
And your story will ring around the world
As people hear from the heart of a girl
Who decided early to seek, to find..., to live!
For through her
Demonstrations of grace will God give!"
It was in the valley she shed the tears
But on the mountain, she found she could stand

And sing!
Smiling as she looked back down through the years
Knowing it was I Who had held her hand
Through everything.
As we traveled together, I told her
That Satan would fall before her
Because of his defeat my Me at Calvary
That he would see our arrival

THOSE MOMENTS THAT MATTER

At our Father's throne of grace
And he would see
The glow upon her face
A glow he would never again erase
Yes, he will see her there
And he will know she won
When he sees her standing beside God's son

It was side by side we traveled
Though she did not always know
For her faith often faltered
And sometimes she did lose her glow
But there was never a time I left her
I had PROMISED to stay
And though she was tempted to wander
She walked with me day by day
It was a memorable journey
Indeed! A time we will not forget
She knows I supplied her every need
And paid her every debt
She knows she is cherished among women
Because I have told her so
She is one for whom I left Heaven
Just to let her know
That is all we ever sought
When with my blood she was bought
God, Our Father and Me
We wanted to set her free

Perfection

She could not reach it
And no one knew how to teach it
But perfect she thought she must be
So, it was grace she had to see
And grace was shown to her repeatedly
Each time there was a big unanswered "why?"
Every single time she could not understand
Each time she wanted to give and die
It was grace that equipped her for each demand
In all things she came to see God's Hand
Yes, through the years
She learned to recognize His Hand
For indeed! It was the Hand of Her God
The Hand of God alone
The Hand of One Who loved her
Who led her all the way home.

AFTERWORD

For those who look at the back of a book first...
(Yep, I do it, too!)
I reckon I've been where the rubber meets the road all my spiritual life.
I started there.
I stayed there.
I like it there.
My strongest influence before school was a mentally, emotionally and spiritually ill grandmother who dabbled in witchcraft and fortune telling.
It fascinated me.
What she did, that is.
Her fascination with me, however, did not fascinate me at all.
She sought to teach me her crafts, as her father before her, had taught her. I sought to understand their origin, but never, ever to practice them. Somehow, I innately knew that they were manipulative ploys and just plain wrong.
Among my earliest memories of my earthbound spiritual journey is a place of rebellion and defiance in my heart, a place to which I constantly withdrew in the face of all my grandmother tried to teach me.
I call that place "where the rubber meets the road." It was there, in that protected place, clearly under the Shadow of His Wings, that I sought, even demanded, to know God.
He met me there.

He still does.

Perhaps it is this background, this personal history, that makes me KNOW that when you seek God with all your heart, God will come to you, even if you never pick up a bible.

The Bible became and remains part of my most treasured resources on my spiritual journey, but God is bigger than that book, or any other resource.

If one would truly seek to know God, then God will be known in Spirit and in Truth. God is unlimited in the ways He chooses to reveal Himself, but yeah... the Bible is a good place to start if you have access to one.

If you are searching today, then I hope that THOSE MOMENTS THAT MATTER will give you the courage to explore your own "moments that matter" in your very personal quest for love, acceptance, truth and peace.

Connect with me please at maryjaneholt.com and tell me about your journey...

~ mjh

THOSE MOMENTS THAT MATTER

Made in the USA
Columbia, SC
29 February 2024